Ripper Notes
The International
Journal for Ripper
Studies

Editor: Dan Norder

Associate Editor:
Wolf Vanderlinden

Address:
Dan Norder, *RN* editor
2 N. Lincoln Ridge Dr.
Apt. #521
Madison, WI 53719

www.RipperNotes.com
dan@norder.com

Subscriptions:
Ripper Notes is
published quarterly in
January, April, July and
October. One year /
four issue subscriptions
cost $40 in the U.S.,
$45 in Canada and the
U.K. and $50 in other
countries. Payment by
check or money order
made out to Dan Norder
and in U.S. funds can
be sent to the address
above, or pay with a
credit card (or PayPal
funds) at our website
www.RipperNotes.com

Those who would rather
pay in British pounds
can send a check for
£25 (U.K.) or £28
(other countries) made
out to Jennifer Pegg to:

Jennifer Pegg
RN subscriptions
81 Rowan Street
Leicester
LE3 9GP
UK

Advertising:
Advertising space costs
$40 per full interior
page. Partial pages and
the back cover are also
available. Contact the
editor for more details.

January 2005 — Issue #21

Contents copyright 2005 by Dan Norder for *Ripper Notes*.
ISBN 0-9759129-2-5
Ripper Notes is published by Inklings Press.

The opinions expressed in articles and letters are those of the individual
authors and are not necessarily shared by the editors.

On the cover: The front is a detail from "Ludgate Hill, Looking from
Fleet Street – The Newspaper Row of London" which ran in an 1897
issue of *Collier's Weekly*. The full image can be seen on the cover of
Alan Sharp's forthcoming *London Correspondence: Jack the Ripper
and the Irish Press*. The first pages of two of the Norman Hastings
news articles are on the back cover. The background for both sides is a
November 10, 1888, report in the *Times* about Mary Jane Kelly's death.

Introduction: Read All About It

Ah, newspapers. I have always loved them, from when I was a child sketching up a front page of an imaginary copy of "Norder News," to college when I spent more time at the student newspaper office than eveywhere else put together. There is nothing else quite like seeing something you wrote, designed or edited come off a press with your name on it. I thought about making a career out of it, but the pay in the field was just too low to really consider. Now I publish and edit this magazine, which I enjoy tremendously.

But when it comes to Ripperology, the newspapers reports are a mixed blessing. We can read all sorts of wonderful details about the case, marvel at the stories witnesses told, and see how Ripper hysteria spread across London and all around the world. Of course the problem is that a large portion of what those accounts claimed about the case turned out to be completely wrong. It wasn't until the late 20th century when authors started getting access to what remained of the original police files that we could start to realize just how much of we thought we knew about the Whitechapel murders was based upon the confusion, speculation and sometimes outright imagination of the journalists of the day. The popular conception of the Ripper is still largely just the character created by the press from long ago. If it weren't for the papers, many of the misconceptions about the case wouldn't exist.

On the other hand, if this mysterious and largely mythical Jack the Ripper hadn't been played up in the news, we may have never even heard of the case today. And in some instances, with the police records as spotty as they are, the old articles are the only things we have to try to fill in some of the gaps of our knowledge.

So it's with that love-hate relationship with the press that I introduce this edition of *Ripper Notes* looking at how the newspapers treated the case.

We start out with Don Souden's examination of just how badly mangled the accounts of Mary Jane Kelly's death were when they reached print; you can use that as something to keep in mind when reading other news articles from the time. Then Alan Sharp writes about the politics involved in the journalists' opinions of how the police led the investigation, with a special emphasis on reports from Ireland (which had very strong political views because of the huge controversy over England's control over that country). Associate Editor Wolf Vanderlinden follows that with a piece spotlighting some specific articles to see what they might tell us about the case.

Then we get into the article at the heart of this issue of *Ripper Notes*: a special in-depth look at the Whitechapel murders, from the early victims now not generally believed to have been killed by the Ripper, through the classic victims of the Autumn of Terror, and then into the aftershocks of the case years later. This is a reprint of a series of articles in 1929 that was rediscovered by Nicholas Connell a while back and now published here for the first time in 75 years. While many of the individual details presented have since been shown to be wrong, and some of the conclusions that author Norman Hastings made don't coincide with modern beliefs on the case, overall the piece is an amazing look at the impact the killings had on society. And, as Hastings claims to have gotten information directly from officers at the time, some of the details might even provide seeds for further research.

After that we have a couple of articles that could be considered follow-ups to our last issue. Prolific Ripper author and scholar Stewart P. Evans returns to these pages with some additional information on the myth that wouldn't die: how psychic R.J. Lees supposedly solved the case with his psychic visions. Jennifer Pegg then fills us in on what happened at the Ghost Club conference on Jack the Ripper.

Then we round things out with Caroline Morris' fun look at the Cloak & Dagger Club's Christmas party, a new feature here reprinting old news articles with added commentary (inspired by this issue's theme but worth doing each time we go to print) and our regular columns. It all adds up to the most pages we've ever run in a single issue (which also explains why the "Heartless" article mentioned last issue as being in this one didn't make it: there just wasn't room for it).

And our growth by leaps and bounds leads us into the next topic of conversation.

Starting with the July 2004 issue we switched to a new format that more than doubled the amount of content in each issue. (While the page dimensions are smaller than they used to be, we also are regularly run three times the number of pages of previous issues, so it comes out to double the number of printed words). When you add up everything you get in a subscription, we give you more in just four issues than our competitors give you in six. Quantity-wise we are at the top of the heap, and when it comes to quality I think we meet our exceed the others as well. And it's not just me: the *Casebook: Jack the Ripper* site recently changed its review of this publication from "second only to *Ripperologist*" to "every bit as good as *Ripperologist*," as one example.

We've been keeping our subscription price the same as it was before all these changes were made, but it's time to bring those more in line with our current situation. After this issue, the base price will be $40 a year instead of $30, with increased costs for mailings to other countries. Because we can print issues in the UK (our experiment last issue worked out well), we can keep UK subscriptions (and Canadian ones too) at only $5 more ($45 – right around what the other major magazine charges for local delivery). Based simply on greater shipping costs, people in other countries will pay $10 extra ($50 total). I'm not sure how everyone will react to the increase, but if you comparison shop I'm sure you'll find that this is still the best bargain out there. We also now let you pay in American dollars or British pounds (see page one for more details).

Oh, and if you check out the cover, you'll see something's missing. (No, I don't mean the fact that this is the first issue in a while that doesn't have a scary-looking Jack the Ripper with scars on his face on the front.) As part of the evolving changes to the publication, we've removed the "American Journal for Ripper Studies" subtitle. This is partly to make the cover more book-like, but it's also a reflection of the fact that my geographic location isn't any more of an influence on the nature of the content than the location of all our other contributors, who come from around the globe. Our authors hail from England, Ireland, Canada, Italy, Australia and Germany, not just the U.S. With the addition of printing facilities in the United Kingdom and the acceptance of payment in British pounds, the days of *Ripper Notes* being a strictly American publication are over, if they ever truly existed in the first place.

On the table of contents page (and on websites and other places where we mention the publication) you'll now see the description: "The International Journal for Ripper Studies." Some people will probably still prefer to consider us "that American magazine," but that won't change who or what we are. We'll still be working to provide a variety of viewpoints from authors all over the world.

Enjoy the issue, and feel free to drop me a line with any questions or comments you might have.

- Dan Norder

The Murder in Cartin's Court

By Don Souden

*Don Souden is a freelance journalist, author and occasional baseball player who lives in Connecticuts's panhandle socket. His latest mystery novel is **The Same ... Only Different.***

Thanks to the telegraph cables that spanned the globe, newspapers around the world were able to bring to their readers on November 10, 1888, the horrible details of a murder that occurred in London the day before. The badly mutilated body of Mary Jane Lawrence, her head severed from her body and placed between her legs, was discovered by friends in an outbuilding of a stable yard known as Cartin's Court. Three bloodhounds were reported to be in hot pursuit of the fiend responsible for the murder, and Metropolitan Police Commissioner Sir Charles Warren was himself on the scene directing operations.

If the previous paragraph seems to be describing a murder with which crime historians are quite unfamiliar there is a good reason for that because it never happened. Yet, that apocryphal story is only an amalgam of some of the many bits of misinformation disseminated by the press in the first few days after the death of Mary Jane Kelly in her room at 13 Miller's Court. Indeed, she was variously identified as Lizzie Fisher, Mary Jane Lawrence, Fair Emma, and "Ginger" as well as Mary Jane Kelly/Marie Jeannette Kelly, while the *Bournemouth Visitors Directory* managed three different forms of Mary Jane Kelly in one short article on November 14.

Similarly, the site of the murder was

November 10, 1888 Illustrated Ripper News *Price*

Another horrible mu
committed in Londo
who has so vexed the
The badly mutilated
Jane Lawrence, foun
WITH HER HEAD S
PLACED BETWEEI
The locality of the la
stable yard known a
Three bloodhounds
in hot pursuit of the
for the murder, and
Police Commissione
Warren – is himsel

How Cartin's Court might have looked in a newspaper.

called Cartin's Court, Mellow Court, Mc-Carthy's Court, Dorset Court and eventually Miller's Court. At least those variations are easily explained. The small court was known colloquially as "McCarthy's Court," and that name could have been slurred into something a reporter's ear rendered as "Cartin's." In the same way, Miller's Court may have sounded like "Mellow" to another reporter unfamiliar with the area. Many of the other mistakes in the initial reports, however, defy comprehension and can only suggest very sloppy work by the journalists involved.

Barnaby and Burgho, the two bloodhounds originally planned to try to track the Ripper before their owner became too concerned about their safety.

Illustration from an 1890 print.

The scene of the crime was sometimes described as being an outbuilding or shed and even many of those stories that correctly reported that the murder happened in a room said it was on the second floor. Then there were the stories that had the murder occurring in a building that was the equivalent of what would today be called a "hot-pillow motel," that is a house of assignation where rooms were rented for the night by amorous couples. That the *Port Phillip* (Australia) *Herald* would make such a suggestion, as far removed from the scene as it was, is possibly pardonable, but the *East London Observer*, on November 10, 1888, reported thusly:

> According to all accounts, the woman who was murdered was not a regular habitué of the place; on the contrary, she was rather well dressed, apparently about twenty-five years of age, and even good looking. As to what time she came to the house on Friday morning, and as to a description of the man who accompanied her, no definite information has been received at the time of writing, thanks to the reticence of the police. This much, however, has been found, that some payment was made by the man for the use of the room; that that payment was received by someone residing in the house; and that the murderer and his victim entered the place in the small hours of Friday morning ....

To the *Observer*'s credit, it did go on to state there were only *two* bloodhounds on the scent. True, they weren't employed at all, but at least the number was correct.

In the same way, *most* of the newspapers got *some* of the details correct, even in their earliest accounts, but overall the quality of the reporting was very bad. Not only were the names of people and places rendered inaccurately, but also all manner of rumors were retold as fact. As a result, stories that continue to frustrate Ripperologists to this day — like the tale that Mary Jane Kelly had a son (described as anywhere from seven- to 11-years-old) living with her — gained immediate currency, and the deeper we dig into newspaper reports the less reliable they become.

The reasons for this sad state of affairs were many, but one important one (already alluded to in the quotation from the *Observer*) was the refusal of the Metropolitan Police to practice anything like modern press relations. The press corps was excluded from crime scenes and given scant information, something that had caused the London *Star* to write after the murders of Stride and Eddowes:

> In New York, where the escape of a murderer is as rare as it is common here, the reporters are far more active agents in ferreting out crime than the detectives. They are no more numerous or more intelligent than the reporters of London, but they are given every facility and opportunity to get all the facts and no part of any case is hidden from them unless the detectives' plan makes it necessary to keep it a secret. The consequence is that a large number of sharp and experienced eyes are focused upon every point of a case, a number of different theories develop which the reporters follow up, and instances in which the detection of a criminal is due to a newspaper reporter are simply too common to create any particular comment ... The sooner the police authorities appreciate and act on this the sooner the Whitechapel fiend will be captured and human life in London rendered a little more safe.

Of course, the *Star* was openly critical of the Metropolitan Police, from Warren down to the lowliest beat-walker, and its description of police-press relations (then or now) in the United States was overly generous. Moreover, its letters columns (and those of rival newspapers) were filled full with theories and suggestions about capturing the Ripper, so there was no dearth of input upon which reporters might act. Further, the way some newspapers would prominently mention detectives relatively low in the hierarchy suggests that they had developed news sources within the department. Finally, the November 10, 1888, *New York Sun* account of the murder, which seems to have been written by its own correspondent, observed archly, "The police do nothing but observe secrecy — a secrecy easily melted with a half crown, by the way."

Nonetheless, most reporters were forced to scramble for whatever information they could obtain from dubious sources and this was never more obvious than in the immediate aftermath of the Kelly murder. Unlike the other murders ascribed to the Ripper, this one was not discovered until nearly mid-day, and that meant the number of the curious drawn to Dorset Street, even with the competing Lord Mayor's Day festivities, was commensurately larger. With reporters specifically excluded from the scene, they had to seek information from anyone claiming knowledge of the deceased — and there seems to have been many in that category.

One of those sources of information was Dr. J. R. Gabe of Mecklenburgh Square, whose name appears in early stories about the murder as one of the physicians immediately called to Miller's Court. The November 10, 1888, *Daily Telegraph* account included: "Dr. J. R. Gabe, who viewed the body, said he had seen a great deal in dissecting rooms, but he had never witnessed such a horrible sight as the murdered woman presented." The first reports of the murder scene in other newspapers were also clearly provided by Gabe, and his comments colored press coverage globally. The details were often graphic. The *New York Herald* quoted him saying, in part: "Below the neck the trunk suggested a sheep's carcass in a slaughter house."

Thus, it is interesting that almost as

quickly as Dr. Gabe's name appeared in print it disappeared. He is not even mentioned in the encyclopedic *The Jack the Ripper A to Z*. The possibility suggests itself that "Dr. Gabe" was, like "Lizzie Fisher," a figment of the imagination or the garbling of another physician's name. However, some recent (and rapid) research by Nina Thomas, Robert Charles Linford and Chris Scott established that John R. Gabe, originally from Wales, was a practicing doctor and "medical official" at 16 Mecklenburgh Square at the time and very likely had been one of the first medical men of the scene. Perhaps his speedy disassociation from the event was occasioned by his loose lips. The police strove to keep as much information as possible secret, and Gabe's willingness to speak with the press probably cast him into their immediate disfavor.

Gabe, however, was the exception for anyone officially connected to the investigation and reporters on the scene had to get information from among their fellow spectators. This was no doubt responsible for the different names initially given the deceased and descriptions that varied from "dark complexioned' to "fair as a lily" as well as the well-publicized story from an acquaintance of the murdered woman that her despair was so great the previous evening that she was contemplating suicide. Great sob-story stuff, but without any attribution and at odds with everything (albeit little) we have come to know about Kelly's character.

Another reason for the pervasiveness and persistence of so much press misinformation was technological advances. Today, with the Internet, cell-phones and real-time satellite television transmission, we daily marvel at how small the world has become. There is no denying that fact, but in our smugness we often forget how shrunken the globe had already become by 1888. The trans-oceanic cables and telegraph land lines meant that news of Mary Kelly's murder reached readers in Atchison, Kansas, or Bismarck, N.D., almost as quickly as it did those in London.

Unfortunately, there was a penalty to be paid for this speedy dissemination of the news. For one thing, the distance from the event meant that the earliest reports, with their initial misinformation, formed the basis for the main stories of an event in most overseas newspapers. And, except for a couple of big-city newspapers, all the reports throughout North America would be culled from the same few sources. Based on several key phrases repeated verbatim, it is probable that most of the newspapers — from the Atchison *Daily Globe* and the Bismarck *Daily Tribune* to the Winnipeg, Canada, *Manitoba Daily Press* — all got their stories from the *New York Times*. There were some exceptions. The *Frederick* (Maryland) *News* and Marion, Ohio, *Daily Star,* among others, appear to have had a different, though common, source, and a few newspapers did have reports filed by their own correspondents in London.

Nonetheless, this commonality of sources for many North American papers (and provincial British ones as well) meant that the same mistakes were broadcast far and wide and because of this gained an undeserved veracity. Moreover, once newspapers printed something about the Ripper murders they seemed to accept its truthfulness themselves and would continue to print those "facts" in subsequent stories.

This was especially so in North America, where most of the newspapers continued to allude to a message supposedly scrawled near Annie Chapman's body: "Five! Fifteen and I give myself up." That this story was totally discredited almost from the moment it was first reported did not deter many editors. Sometimes they also got their facts scrambled, as when the *Frederick Herald* mentioned in its first Kelly story that earlier Ripper victim Annie Chapman had been "stabbed 39 times," a fate that had actually befallen Martha Tabram. Even the London newspapers, however, were not immune to failing to keep up with the news and the *Star* of November 10, 1888, still identified Catherine Eddowes as "Kelly," the surname first attached to her.

Finally, some of the blame for the plethora of Ripper reporting errors must be laid at the feet of the newspapers themselves. There was certainly no lack of competition, with some 15 morning, nine evening and 35 weekly newspapers readily available in London. Nor did the newspapers lack incentive, for a Jack the Ripper murder was a story guaranteed to sell as many copies as could be printed. That said, however, a perusal of the press coverage of the Ripper's murder spree suggests a low tolerance for accuracy, a lack of initiative, a herd instinct (even a certain docility) and, worst of all, coverage in all too many instances that was driven by political considerations.

In regard to the first charge, inaccuracy, the *Star* was quite open about its approach when it wrote in its Nov. 10 issue: "The desire to be interesting has had its effect on the people who live in the Dorset-street-court and lodging-houses, and for whoever cares to listen there are A HUNDRED HIGHLY CIRCUMSTANTIAL STORIES, which, when carefully sifted, prove to be totally devoid of truth" [emphasis in original]. And, having said that, the *Star* then went on to recount all those false stories. Of possible interest to modern researchers, one of those stories said to be fallacious was Elizabeth Prater's account of hearing a cry of "murder" in the wee hours of the morning.

As for a general lack of initiative, there were some few enterprising journalists who managed to ferret out information on their own, but those leads seem never to have been followed up and developed. Or, if they were and proved to be dead ends, readers were never informed (thus providing endless fodder for future theorists). The *Star* staff was perhaps the most energetic in following up on stories, but then it was also among the more sensationalist. It was also the most critical of Sir Charles Warren and certainly had every hope of embarrassing the man and his department. The newspaper did seek out and interview both Israel Schwartz and George Hutchinson, but the resulting stories are so detailed in certain parts as to suggest the frequent use of leading questions to make a point. The inescapable conclusion is that the newspapers were simply reactive throughout the fall of 1888.

The herd instinct is often apparent by the similarity of story themes in the various newspapers, even those that had their own reporters on the ground. This was almost certainly the result of freely using Press Association boilerplate. An instance is that on November 10 the *Daily Telegraph, Manchester Guardian, Star* and *St. James Gazette* (and likely other newspapers as well) all had stories about a possible link between the dates of the murders and the regular arrival of cattle boats from the Continent. The stories were not identical and gave no attribution for the theory, but it clearly came from a single source that influenced all the newspapers. Perhaps Edward Knight Larkins, who several weeks later would begin bombarding the Home Office with letters and charts on the topic, provided the Press Association with an early draft of his theory.

As for my suggestion of docility on the part of the newspapers, the handling of the statement of self-proclaimed witness George Hutchinson is a case in point. In his statement to the police, Hutchinson specifically mentioned the man he saw had a "Jewish appearance." The local newspapers, however, changed "Jewish" to "foreign." Since several American newspapers that carried Hutchinson's statement used the word Jewish, the inference is that the change was not made by the police before release but by the newspapers. Perhaps it was an example of "journalistic ethics" (a phrase that would strike many as an oxymoron on a par with "military intelligence") and a bit of self-censorship in order to avoid inflaming anti-Semitic tensions, or it may have been mandated by the police. In either case it suggests a willingness to be cowed on the part of so many newspapers that otherwise protested a fierce independence.

That brings up the final aspect of my criticism of much of the coverage: reporting driven by a political agenda. The reasons for that agenda and the details of the political controversies at work are well beyond the scope of this article. Suffice it to say that many of the London newspapers at the time were quite openly aligned with one political party or another, and a series of political events in Britain at the time resulted in several different factions all wanting to bring disrepute upon Sir Charles Warren and the Metropolitan Police. This animosity colored some of the coverage — even to the extent that some may well have thought an unsolved series of horrific murders was politically advantageous — and that is never a good situation.

Nor should the American papers, especially those with their own correspondents on the scene, be exempted from this criticism. While not being particularly involved in the parochial political squabbles that animated their British brethren, American newspapers never passed up a chance to "twist the English lion's tail." Thus, the *Boston Globe* was eager to refer as the Lord Mayor's Day as an "annual nuisance," the Washington, D.C. *Evening Star* wrote that the London policemen were generally dull and stupid and the *Brooklyn* (New York) *Daily Eagle* went so far as to write: "Much more reasonable would it be to infer that the murderer is a member or ex-member of the London police force ..."

A more veiled criticism appeared the same day (November 10) in *The New York Sun*, which ran an interview with Superintendent William Murray of the New York City police, who said:

Thomas Byrnes

From his book *Professional Criminals of America,* **1886**

I presume that the London Police are doing the very best they can and will ultimately unravel the mystery ... I am confident, though, that no such crime could continue under the system of the New York police. The entire force would, if necessary, be sent out in citizen's dress to run down the assassin.

The *New York Herald* on November 10 interviewed Chief Inspector Thomas Byrnes of the New York City police, who uttered much the same sentiments:

All I will say ... is that such a continuous wholesale slaughter could never take place in this city without having the fiend delivered up to justice .... well, I'm glad the fellow is not in this city, but if he were I think I'd trace him to his lair if it kept me and my men without sleep for weeks.

The *Herald* also quoted an American tourist in London as saying, "After this, I shall never grumble at any error of our New York Police." This is rather ironic because the same issue also carried an item —quite laudatory in tone — about a particularly egregious bit of police brutality by a New York policeman that was directed toward a hapless burglar caught in the act.

Having gotten this far in a study of press coverage, there still remains the question of how useful the contemporary newspaper reports are. The simple answer, unfortunately, is not very useful. This study arose from a spirited discussion of the events after the arrival of the police at 13 Miller's Court on November 9, 1888. Some of the stories by newspapers like the *Times, Daily Telegraph* and *Manchester Guardian,* while not without some errors, are quite good and accord well with the facts as we know them. Yet they provide little additional information than what is available from the inquest testimony or (at least in the case of Kelly) the witnesses' statements to the police.

There is an old joke about a policeman coming upon a drunk crawling on his knees underneath a street lamp. The policeman asks the drunk what he's doing and the drunk tells him he's looking for his wallet. The policeman then asks if he remembers losing his wallet by the lamp and the drunk replies: "No shir, I dropped it down the shtreet, but (hic) the light is sho much brighter here." That is too often what we face with newspaper articles about Jack the Ripper: They aren't very helpful, but there's a lot of them out there, and they're pretty easy to get at as well.

Still, if the drunk wasn't very likely to find his wallet under the street lamp, he just might have found something else worthwhile, and so too might we find something interesting and instructive in the old newspapers even if hard facts are elusive. And that is exactly what happened while I was poring over news stories about the Mary Jane Kelly case. Nothing earth-shattering, to be sure, but there are a few items worth pondering in the future.

I'll begin with one that is somewhat humorous, but also makes an important point. In the same November 10 issue of the *New York Herald* that carried reports about the Kelly murder there was a story about Mrs. Flora Wright of 110 West 32nd Street in New York who actually found a man under her bed when preparing for sleep. She took one look and went racing into the street screaming, "Jack the Ripper! Jack the Ripper! The Ripper's under my bed!"

Whoever it was who first signed a letter Jack the Ripper was a marketing genius that modern companies with all their emphasis on "product branding" can only dream of equaling. The Ripper name's first appearance in a London newspaper was on October 1, and a little more than a month later it had crossed the Atlantic Ocean to become such a pervasive term that the first reaction of a woman who finds a man under her bed in Manhattan is to think that he's Jack the Ripper. And, as an example of how quickly the language of popular culture could cross "the Pond" back then, it might render meaningless the efforts of some to gain insights from any Americanisms in the Ripper letters.

Moving to the slightly more serious, what would a Ripper article be without at least some speculative theories? I make no guarantees about any of these and I only advance them as fuel for future thought on a cold winter's night. Still, a couple of ideas did arise from all the stories I read, such as the early emergence of "Lizzie Fisher" and, more particularly, "Mary Jane Lawrence."

Although there are some who still want to see the workings of a murky conspiracy in the initial misidentification of Kelly as "Lizzie Fisher," it seems established that Fisher was another woman altogether who was confused with Kelly by an early source used by both the Press Association and the *New York Times* (and through the latter repeated by many newspapers in North America). It seems likely that "Mary Jane Lawrence" was another early misidentification provided to a correspondent for some other American newspapers.

However, as long as we are having a little fun, let us take it a little further. The newspapers in America, even with the benefit of the time difference, had to go with the earliest reports in order to publish on November 10. That meant reporters had to file stories while much was still unknown, including the name of the victim. Imagine then a reporter as part of the crowd surrounding Miller's Court, everyone eager to find out who was murdered. Suddenly, someone hears, "it's Mary Jane," and someone else immediately tells a questioning reporter, "Oh, it must be Mary Jane *Lawrence*," and that name gets wired across the Atlantic.

There is nothing unusual or even startling about that surmise, and it fits well with what we think we know about the Lizzie Fisher identification. But just maybe there was a Mary Jane Lawrence (or someone who went by that name) dossing in the area. And what if it was this Mary Jane who Caroline Maxwell ran into the morning of November 9? After all, Mrs. Maxwell admitted she scarcely knew Kelly, but did address the woman she saw that morning as "Mary Jane" and that greeting was acknowledged. That she was actually addressing

Mary Jane Lawrence could answer a few lingering questions.

Then there is the business of "Marie Jeanette Kelly." Barnett told everyone that Kelly preferred that name to plain Mary Jane, but that preference seems to have begun and ended with Joe. Read all the early interviews, even with her professed friends, and they all called her Mary Jane. It wasn't until Joe began to talk that Mary became *Marie*. She may have liked the sound of Marie, but it seems an affectation only Joe was willing to indulge.

For those who like their speculation really off-the-wall, there was an item that ran in the November 10 *Boston Globe* that told readers [emphasis in original]:

> Profiting by former blunders, the police called a photographer to take a picture of the room before the body was removed from it. This gives rise to a report that bloody **Handwriting Was on the Wall,** though three or four people who were allowed to enter the room say they did not observe it, but possibly they were too excited to notice details.

However, before any "Maybrickites" go into ecstasies it should be mentioned that whatever its repute today, the *Globe* was a much different paper in 1888, one prone to questionable journalistic practices. Several years after printing the Ripper-writing rumor it would get into serious trouble for running a totally disreputable story that Lizzie Borden slew her parents because they had discovered she was pregnant.

Finally, one more little speculative nugget mined from the Kelly coverage. There were several interviews published with people who seemed to know her well enough that their facts jibe with what we know, except they all said that while Mary Jane looked to be 30 years old she was actually in her mid-20s. Well, her profession and propensity for alcohol could age one prematurely, but vanity can just as easily take the years off. With so little luck so far finding any birth records for a Mary Jane Kelly, it might just prove profitable to set back the birth date at least a few years.

For all the interesting little items found in my study, however, the overriding conclusion is that the contemporary newspaper articles must be treated with considerable skepticism, no matter how exciting some stories may seem. When a newspaper prints a dozen things as "fact" that we know are demonstrably wrong, to eagerly seize upon a 13th just because it says what we want to believe is, as Dr. Johnson once said about a second marriage, "the triumph of hope over experience."

It seems only fair, though, to let a newspaper have the last word. In its November 10 story about the Kelly murder *The Eastern Post and City Chronicle* concluded by saying, "First reports, however, are always more or less conflicting." Amen.

The London Police:
The View from the Irish Press

By Alan Sharp

Alan Sharp is a writer, theatre director and freelance IT expert in Dublin, Ireland. His book **London Correspondence: Jack the Ripper and the Irish Press** *(Ashfield Press) is scheduled to be released in February.*

On August 31st, 1888, Mary Ann "Polly" Nichols became the third victim of the Whitechapel murders. This is a statement of fact, and not as you may have surmised an attempt to begin a discussion on whether or not the Ripper had taken any victims before Polly. The fact is that whether Emma Smith and Martha Tabram were Ripper victims or not, they were murders number one and two in the series, according to the newspapers of 1888.

This is an important fact to remember. Martha Tabram's murder garnered very little by way of press coverage and almost none overseas. Emma Smith fared even less well. Aside from the local press such as the *East London Advertiser* and the *Eastern Post and City Chronicle*, this was a murder which passed almost unremarked upon by the newspapers of the day. But it is because of these two earlier murders that we have such a wealth of material available to us in the local, national and international press from the week following Nichol's murder. If this had been an isolated incident it would probably have received as little attention as the earlier cases. The reason it did not was because it was regarded as the third in the series.

By the time the Ripper murders came along, London's radical Socialist evening newspaper the *Star* had already begun a campaign to oust Sir Charles Warren, the

Chief Commissioner of the Metropolitan Police, from office. On the very day of the Nichols murder they published a lengthy editorial on the subject of his fitness for command, which concluded that "if a vote of the people of London could be held in a

matter in which they ought to have the determining voice, Sir Charles would not remain another week in the position he has so grossly abused." As the murders continued, criticism of Warren and his force would spread to other newspapers and other countries, but it was *The Star* which stole a jump on all of them. On September 1st, just a day after the murder, they published their first intimation that Warren might be unfit to lead the hunt for the killer. "When Sir Charles has done quarrelling with his detective service," they wrote, "he will perhaps help the citizens of East London to catch him."

One ever present element of pretty much ever Ripper book written in the last hundred years has been a commentary on the efficiency of the police force, and particularly of the Metropolitan police. Although in recent years this has tended to comprise a well-reasoned investigation, and the likes of Paul Begg and Philip Sugden have defended the actions of Warren and his force, many writers particularly in the earlier years bought in utterly to the idea of their incompetence. Donald McCormick said of Warren that he was "a most unsuitable choice for the office" and that he was "unimaginitive, authoritarian, incapable of assessing any problem except in military terms, he upset the entire police force by his tactlessness and antagonized the Criminal Investigation Department by his scant regard for that body," while Tom Cullen said of his appointment that it was "little short of a national disaster." The attitude is still in evidence today, with Patricia Cornwell stating that "ridding London of Warren may be the only good deed Jack the Ripper did."

These writers have been mostly taking their lead from newspaper reports in the likes of the *Star* and the *Pall Mall Gazette,* and to a lesser extent the *Daily Telegraph.* It should be remembered, however, that the first two of these had a radical agenda to uphold, and Warren had blotted his own copybook with his actions in regard to the Trafalgar Square riots the previous year. Warren was portrayed by them as a tool of the Conservative Government, although in fact nothing could have been further from the truth. His many disagreements with the Home Secretary Henry Matthews are well documented, and it is seldom remembered that Warren was in fact an appointment of Hugh Childers, Matthews' predecessor in Gladstone's Liberal Government. Warren was in fact a lifelong Liberal with surprisingly progressive views, but he was also a man of principle who believed that his professional duty was to uphold the laws of the land regardless of his own personal opinions.

It wasn't only the London press who poured reprobation upon the heads of Warren and his men. The *New York Times* reported that "the London police and detective force is probably the stupidest in the world" and that "they confess themselves without a clue, and they devote their entire energies to preventing the press from getting at the facts." Washington's *Evening Star* said, "The stupid London police have been chasing him for more than a year with no hope of success," and the *Montreal Daily Star* stated, "Not one of the persons arrested on suspicion has been connected with the remotest circumstances that could induce belief that he was even aware that the murder had been committed, and the police would have been as thoroughly justified in arresting the Queen herself as they were in taking into custody the persons they were compelled to set at liberty for want of evidence."

However, once again we can assign motive to these utterances. North America was still thought of as the "New World," and both countries liked to think of themselves as modern and progressive, a far cry from the old fashioned, outmoded traditionalists of the British Isles. The press, then as now, writes what the public wants to hear, and the public wanted to hear how much better protected they were than their British counterparts.

Ireland was a special case. Here we had a country that was still under direct British rule and which was divided between those struggling for independence and those who remained loyal to the Crown. It might have been thought that the opinions expressed on the London police, as representatives of Crown authority, might have been divided on the same lines, but a study of the press of the day shows that this was patently not the case.

One factor which clouded the issue, at least as far as the Nationalist press were concerned, was the resignation of James Monro in the weeks prior to the Polly Nichols murder. Under normal circumstances one might have expected the Home Rulers to use any opportunity to attack Warren, especially as it had been his prohibition of a protest at the prison treatment of Nationalist MP William O'Brien which had led to the events of Bloody Sunday. However, Monro, who as well as his duties as chief of the CID was also in charge of the secret Irish department, Section D, the forerunner to the Special Branch, was an even greater target for their scorn. The *Freeman's Journal* welcomed his resignation in their leader column of September 1st:

It is satisfactory to find that there is a pretty unanimous feeling among the London police that Sir Chas Warren's policy in Scotland Yard, which only last week brought about the resignation of Mr. Monro, the Assistant Commissioner, will have the effect of abolishing the Criminal Investigation Department or crippling its usefulness very materially. If any such result follows on Sir Chas Warren's action all decent men will be ready to support the Chief Commissioner instead of holding aloof as they do now. The Criminal Investigation Department was up to some years ago a very useful institution in a big city like London, and it would continue always to be regarded as such if its functions were confined to the investigation of crime. But latterly it as been converted into a sort of political bureau. The hunt after the dynamiters completely demoralised it. Mr. Monro and his detectives, instead of confining their attentions to the men who come to London to blow up bridges, made a set upon all Irish Nationalists. They followed and dogged men who have as hearty abhorrence of crime as themselves. They swarmed about the House of Commons for the past two sessions, subjecting Irish members to the most offensive form of espionage, and creating such a scandal that English members like Mr. Bradlaugh and Sir Wilfrid Lawson avowed with shame from their places in the house that no such humiliating spectacle could be seen in any capital in Europe. This being the sort of work done by the Criminal Investigation Department, nobody will regret that Sir Charles Warren has given it a knock on the head. What would have pleased Mr. Monro was to be left a perfectly free hand at Whitehall-place, and to be allowed to do as he liked with his detectives and plain clothes policemen. Evidently Sir Charles Warren has very different notions. Sir Charles Warren is a very stern man, and his action in connection with Trafalgar-square shows that he cares very little for the rights of the public in the matter of open meetings, but still he has strong and not altogether objectionable views about the duty of every individual policeman under his charge.

A similar sentiment was expressed in the *Waterford Citizen* of the previous day:

Mr. Monro has endeavoured to build up sensations out of the supposed connection between some of the Irish Nationalists and the dynamiters, and it was believed that he sought to model the London police after the Dublin Castle model. It is hateful to the ordinary Englishman's mind to find a policeman who should be his servant converted into the tool of the Government of the day for political purposes. Sir Charles Warren, notwithstanding his many mistakes, sympathises with this feeling, and Mr. Monro's action did not, therefore, commend his approval. As London would not have these methods at any price, may we hope that Ireland will now be relieved of them?

The previous year had been the jubilee of Queen Victoria, and it had fallen to Monro and his department to uncover a Fenian plot to assassinate the monarch by use of a dynamite attack on Westminster Abbey. Monro, having traced the plot to a consumptive American gentleman named Mr Joseph Cohen, and from him to two men who had visited him shortly before he had succumbed to his illness, he then found that these two men had been invited into the Houses of Parliament and shown around by a Nationalist MP, Mr Joseph Nolan. At Cohen's inquest, Monro announced that Cohen had been a member of the terrorist Clan-na-Gael movement, and had been operating under orders from leading Fenian General Frank Millen. The next day Monro had gone into further detail when talking to press reporters, naming Nolan as a man that had dealings with the dynamitards and with Millen himself, whose daughters he had also welcomed into the House of Commons.

Following this it seems that the police had been keeping a close eye not only on Nolan, but also on all of the members of the Irish Parliamentary Party. That this was still occurring during the time of the Ripper murders is evidenced by this comment from the London Correspondent of the *Cork Examiner* from October 2nd:

It is a curious fact that in spite of the disgraceful break down of the Metropolitan police as detectors of crime, Home Secretary Mathews still insists upon a large number of detectives shadowing the Irish members when they are in town. I walked along the Strand with an Irish member to-night and two detectives followed us all the way. The cost of the two or three hundred men who are employed upon Irish detective force in England ought really to be added to the Irish estimates in order that the British public may have an accurate estimate of the cost of governing Ireland against the will of her people.

So, bizarrely, it seems that Sir Charles Warren, despite being regarded as the enemy of the radical, Home Rule supporting press in England, was treated the exact opposite by their counterparts in Ireland, at least for the time being. Indeed the entire situation seems to have been reversed, with the staunchly Loyalist *Kerry Evening Post* going on the offensive against him on September 5th:

> The retirement of Mr. Monro, C.B., from Scotland Yard causes much speculation. It is an open secret that Sir Charles Warren is not popular amongst either the rank and file or the officials of the Metropolitan force. It is easy to understand this. A soldier was deliberately set at the head of the police with the object of introducing a nearer approach to military discipline. A change was not likely to be accomplished without creating at least temporary ill-feeling. Previous Chief Commissioners, and notably the last, were easy going men. So long as no glaring errors were committed they were content. But Sir Charles Warren demands a new measure of alertness and promptness. He is particular about trifles. He "pokes his nose," as the men say, into every department; and orders about the superior officers in a peremptory manner which would pass as a matter of course in the camp or barrack, but which is new in the dingy offices of Scotland Yard. Mr Monro's retirement is believed to be due to personal friction. It has been known for some time that he and Sir Charles did not "get on." The post of Assistant Commissioner was not an easy one to fill up. Mr. Monro has for several years been specially concerned in tracking out the dynamite conspiracy. His knowledge of its secret ramifications was displayed no doubt for a purpose in connection with the doings of General Millen and his daughters. It is with reference to work in this particular department that an Irish barrister, who has served for some years in the Home Office, has been selected as Mr. Monro's successor.

With the Parnell Commission, an inquiry into allegations by the Times newspaper into connections between Charles Stewart Parnell's Irish Party and the terrorist Fenian Brotherhood and Clan-na-Gael organisations, commencing during the height of the Ripper crimes, the *Freeman's*

Journal on November 20th suggested that this also had a bearing on Monro's resignation:

> It is now said that Sir Chas Warren objected to the action of Mr. Monro in utilising the detective force in working up the *Times* case both because he thought it was improper employment of their services and because it led to their neglect of other more important work. Mr. Monro's position would be quite untenable under such a charge.

In truth, the *Freeman* may well have been doing Monro a disservice. In a letter to his son from Darjeeling in 1904, Monro gave as the real reason for his resignation that he "had refused to do what he considered to be wrong." Monro was indeed under pressure from the Government to assist the *Times* in assembling their case, and it is possible that this is what he was referring to.

For the Nationalist press, the Ripper crimes presented an opportunity. For years past the ordinary peasant Irish had been presented in the leading English journals and in the Loyalist press in Ireland in a poor light. The sense was that, in supporting the cause of such organisations as the Land League and the National League, both prohibited organisations under the law, and in carrying out campaigns of boycotting and the Plan of Campaign, they were acting in a criminal manner. The Plan of Campaign had been instituted the year before, a systematic refusal by tenants to pay what were considered extortionate rents to their landlords. This campaign had led to mass tenant evictions, which in its turn led to what became known as moonlighting campaigns, whereby the bailiffs and emergencymen involved in the evictions, and often tenants who refused to join the campaign, found themselves subject to late night visits under the cover of darkness, sometimes for the purposes of intimidation, sometimes of physical assault and even murder.

This situation had led to the Secretary of State for Ireland, Arthur Balfour, the nephew of Prime Minister Lord Salisbury, to institute the latest in a series of what were known as "Coercion Acts," emergency powers given to the Resident Magistrates, or Removables as they were known. The sense of the act was that the Irish could not be trusted, that they turned a blind eye to crime and coerced others into doing the same, and the special powers allowed for people to be arrested not merely for committing the crime, but also for making statements which appeared to be in approval of or giving encouragement to the criminals. The *Kilkenny Journal* of September 8th commented on the irony of this attitude by a country which had just been subject to a series of horrific and unsolved murders in the East End:

> The Irish are such a nation of savages that ordinary laws are not sufficient to curb their brutal instincts, and the English Government is compelled to step in, and for the sake of humanity strive to stamp out the vice that appears to have settled in this country. Such is the story that would be told by the true blue supporter of Bloody BALFOUR. Now it seems as if the English Government would be conferring a greater benefit upon humanity if it looked nearer home.

Not only did the Ripper crimes give the Nationalists a reason to turn their focus back onto the criminality of England, but it also provided the opportunity to turn the spotlight on a host of other crimes occurring around the country. The *Nationalist* newspaper on September 8th noted the following:

> The London evening sheets are ghastly reading. As one of them puts it, the assassins are crowding the politicians out of the papers. On Monday night they reported such a feast of horrors as the inquest in the Whitechapel mystery, a child murder at Birmingham, a wife murder at Liverpool, the Poplar murder, the attempted murder and suicide by a Wrexham magistrate, the poisoning of a woman on Clapham Common, not to mind a score or so of less tragic and sensational atrocities.

Meanwhile the *Kilkenny Journal*, in the same article quoted above, continued on to say:

> Day after day, until the heart sickens and the mind becomes hardened to the tales of terror, we see in the English papers reports of outrages committed in that country that are enough to bring down the vengeance of God upon the land. In Ireland if a policeman receives a bucket of tar upon his devoted head, or a sheriff's bailiff is compelled to swallow an amount of blue documents which he may find some difficulty in digesting, the British Press howl for "more Coercion," and declare that Ireland should be sunk under the sea. But the same Briton who pens that twaddle at his desk will probably read, without the slightest feeling of horror, how a labourer had roasted his wife or dashed the brains out of several of his children.

Throughout the case criticism was mostly levelled at the superior officers of the force, at Warren, at Monro's successor Dr Robert Anderson, and frequently at the Home Secretary. It was generally accepted that the rank and file of the police were a decent group of men doing a difficult job. However, even early in the case, the newspapers carried stark warnings of what could be expected should the crimes not be detected. The *Cork Examiner* on September 10th commented:

> The former laxity and the present helplessness of the police are exasperating to the dwellers in Whitechapel, and unless the authorities promptly lay their hands on the perpetrator of these appalling crimes there may be trouble in store for us down there. Perhaps the Whitechapel public might themselves do not a little to aid the police in their difficult task. They might propose an effective reward, and they might strengthen the watch on obvious lines of co-operation. Anyhow the police are on their mettle, and it will be an incalculable misfortune if they should be found wanting. All eyes are on Scotland Yard, and it is devoutedly to be hoped that the dastardly villain or wretched monomaniac may be captured before he has an opportunity to add another hapless wretch to the lamentable list of his victims.

The *Ballymena Observer* on September 14th noted:

> The police are being abused with might and main for their failure to find the murderer before now, but it should be remembered that the Whitechapel criminal class is so numerous that the detectives task in getting at a particular individual is a specially difficult one. Besides, it is

by no means clear that these foul deeds were committed by a person belonging to what is usually called the criminal class.

The *Freeman's Journal* of the same day were rather more vehement in their criticism:

> The police have not yet captured the Whitechapel murderer. All their scouring through the East End has failed to give them any clue whatever as to the whereabouts of this fiend. This humiliating failure has heightened the dissatisfaction and indignation which have existed for the past few days throughout London in connection with these terrible crimes. It is now certain that the last murder was committed close to six o'clock in the morning, when there must have been broad daylight. Obviously, from the nature of the murder, the murderer must have been stained all over with blood. He could not have walked very far without being noticed. Nobody, however, seems to have noticed him, and therefore the conjecture is that his lodgings was close at hand. This is an important fact, but so far the police have not been able to make any use of it.

On the other hand, as reported here in the *Dublin Evening Mail* of September 26th, the police were not slow at turning their criticism back on the press themselves:

> Speaking of the Whitechapel murders, it reminds me that many of the police of that unsavoury locality are greatly incensed against everybody and everything associated with "those horrid newspapers." Their lives, they declare, have been made a misery by the incessant importunities and cross-questionings of a small army of reporters. Two of these energetic gentlemen openly boast of having each of them interviewed over two thousand police officer and others, with a view to obtaining "fresh facts."

In fact Sir Charles Warren and other superior officers of the force had become so disenchanted with the constant criticism and carping of the press, together with the demands they made on the time of the officers, that he had given out general orders that no policeman was to give out the slightest information to reporters. For this reason, the truth is that most of the time the newspapers had no idea what kind of activity was taking place within the force. The same newspaper gave some details on September 28th:

> The police remain silent under extreme penalties in the event of divulging the least scrap of information. It is known, however, that they are working indefatigably. Two medical students, at different London hospitals, inform me that there is not an institution of the kind that has not been visited, and where the most careful inquiries have not been instituted. I hear, further, that numerous telegrams have passed between Scotland Yard and the police in America, and that on the other side of the Atlantic a vigorous search has been started with a view, if possible, to discover the whereabouts of the mysterious stranger whose extraordinary demands at the London hospitals may truthfully be said to have astonished the world.

Some policemen did speak to the press however, albeit usually anonymously. It would have been difficult to hold their tongues when they were constantly under fire from the newspapers. The *Morning News* of September 11th printed the views of one officer:

> I was speaking to an officer of Scotland Yard yesterday who has great experience, and he informed me that this case was one of the most difficult class that the police have to deal with. If the crimes are committed by a single individual, who works alone, it is always much more difficult to detect than if a whole gang were concerned. The difficulties are increased in this case, as everything seems to point to the criminal being a debased, morose, taciturn, and half-crazy creature, with considerable cunning and daring.

By the end of September the furore had mostly died down, the attention span of the Irish public having waned and moved on to more lurid fare within their own shores. Reporting picked up for a few days after Coroner Baxter's alarming statement during the summing up of the Annie Chapman inquest, but for the most part the newspapers scarcely mentioned the murders, and when they did it was only to report the arrest and release of yet another unfortunate innocent.

The events of September 30th changed all that, and by the time the following days newspapers appeared they were thick with the details of the double murder and with comment, opinion and theory. It wasn't long before the police were being made the target of their scorn once more. The *Irish Times*, a journal which tried to walk the tightrope between the Nationalists and the Loyalists, was to become one of the most vehement critics of Warren and his men. On October 1st the leader column comprised a lengthy diatribe against the force, stating, among other things:

> The police appear to have been from the first utterly at fault. We think that they are justly blamed for want of knowledge, want of ingenuity, and want of grasp and resource. They appear to have got no clue, or if they found any they have let it slip.

And the following day they continued in much the same vein:

> It surely is an experience of the most appalling description that in these latter days of the Nineteenth Century – when there is in existence a trained army of officials under the direct control and government of the State, provided with practically unlimited opportunities of tracing the courses of the evil-doer and penetrating the inmost recesses of his haunts of wickedness – the sight of policemen and of the detective should be so short as to be unable to follow at no remote distance the bloodstained footsteps of the murderer whose surpassing daring and recklessness set upon his brow the awful and recognisable mark of CAIN.

However, the involvement of the City police following the murder of Catherine Eddowes did not invite the same reprobation. A clue to why this should be appeared in the same October 2nd edition of the *Irish Times*:

> The conduct of the City Police authorities in contradistinction with that of the Metropolitan Police in connection with the latest discovered murders is being freely commented

on by all sections of the Press. The murder in Mitre square being within the city boundaries proper comes under the jurisdiction of the city police, who have given every facility to the Press in their unpleasant labours; while their metropolitan brethren who have charge of the Berner street outrage are by no means, it is said, anxious to assist newspaper men, but on the other hand rather frustrate them in their inquiries.

Once again it was those in command of the force who came in for the lions share of the press disapproval. Henry Matthews – never a popular man in Ireland particularly among the Nationalists who considered him, as a member of the Conservative "enemy," to be a traitor to his Irish Catholic heritage – had encountered the animosity of the rest of the populace as a result of his refusal to grant a reward for the apprehension of the killer. The *Cork Examiner* on October 2nd printed a damning attack:

> That such incompetency as is displayed by Home Secretary Matthews and Sir Charles Warren, the Commissioner, should be allowed to continue unchecked is only proof of how the interests of the country are sacrificed to party exigencies. Mr Matthews was very skilful in bludgeoning the unemployed in Trafalgar Square. For ordinary police duties the force for which he is responsible has utterly broken down. Even the Tory *Daily Telegraph* to-day demands the dismissal of the incompetent Minister, the renegade on Irish affairs, the turncoat in Irish politics.

Belfast's *Morning News* on the same day printed its own take on events:

The indignation of the public against the Home Secretary for declining to offer a reward for the discovery of the Whitechapel murderer is becoming so fierce that it is almost certain that the Government will have to get rid of Mr. Matthews. Mr. Matthews may have been justified in not offering a reward, but the public want some victim, and Mr. Matthews' sins in other directions are so numerous that he can scarcely withstand the present storm.

The *Dublin Evening Mail*, on the other hand, the most loyal of all the Loyalist press, continually resisted jumping onto the bandwagon and gave the government its full support. On October 3rd they seemed to suggest that, far from the police being incompetent, it was the victims themselves who were to blame:

It does not seem to have occurred to anybody that the murders could be effectively stopped by the unfortunate women themselves who are in danger. Let them turn to an honest trade. Even choring would be better than being murdered. That is the way we should suggest for them – in the default of the police – to defend their humble homes and persons. If nobody will be found to employ them, they can take shelter in a workhouse. Even that is better than being murdered. They will not need in that case to be in the streets, and in the most dangerous corners of them, at hours when there is no witness to protect them. The abuse showered on the London police seems to us ridiculous. The police cannot be everywhere. The public cannot afford to keep an officer permanently stationed in every blind alley and accessible

courtyard in London; and the demand that this expense should be undertaken for the protection of a disgusting and demoralising trade, marks an extremely low level of intelligence. It is a moral certainty that the police, from the highest to the lowest, are doing their level best to detect the murderer, and to prevent a repetition of his crimes.

Similarly the *Belfast & Newry Standard* on October 5th voiced their support for the London forces of Law and order:

The police have been sorely blamed, their officers attacked, and popular indignation has more than once gone beyond the region of reason .... On calmly reflecting upon all the incidents of this sanguinary chapter of unexampled crime, it is difficult to discover in what respect the constabulary have failed to discharge their duty of guarding the lives of Londoners to the utmost of their ability, and no unbiased persons will seriously deny that the policemen at the call of Scotland-yard or the Old Jewry would risk their lives at any moment to get hold of the miscreant or miscreants concerned in the murders.

Two days after the double event, the police were dealt yet another crushing blow. Another body was discovered, this time apparently right under their very noses. The Whitehall torso discovery must have had a devastatingly humiliating effect on their sensibilities, and having their noses rubbed in it by the press, as in this example from the *Morning News*, cannot have helped:

If the murder was committed elsewhere the removal of the body to a building about to be used as the headquarters of the police authorities, would seem to suggest that the murderer desired to practice a piece of grim and ghastly humour at the expense of the force that has shown itself so woefully inefficient in discovering the monster who has thrown London into such a ferment.

The month of October would see the opening of the Parnell Commission, and it was noticeable during this month that much of the criticism focused not so much on the police themselves, but on comparisons between the conditions in England and Ireland. The *Cork Examiner* on October 6th had this to say:

Matthews and Warren are thoroughly discredited in the eyes of the public, but they are such useful tools in the hands of the classes in suppressing the movements of the Democracy in London that the Government are unwilling to sacrifice them to the public clamour .... One result of the general outburst of crime in London will be probably this that Mr Cunninghame Graham, Mr Conybeare, or some other British member may be tempted to introduce a Coercion Bill in the autumn for the purpose of preventing brutal crime and outrage in England.

The idea of "Coercion for England" was a constant suggestion of the Nationalist press, and the more radical newspapers were more than happy to use the murders as a an excuse to "vent their spleen." Of all the journals there was none so radical as the *United Ireland*. Owned by Charles Stewart Parnell and edited by William O'Brien, this newspaper had been prohibited from sale under the Coercion Act, and several newssellers had been arrested and imprisoned.

On September 29th they made their feelings on the issue most forcefully felt:

Supposing the Whitechapel assassinations had taken place in Kerry what a universal outcry there would be about the inate depravity and brutality of the Irish race. There has been nothing in Kerry, with all the fierce provocation to which the wretched inhabitants are subjected, a hundred-part as brutal as these purposeless crimes. There would be no loss for a motive in Ireland. The assassinations, it would be taken for granted, were committed at "the secret orders" of a savage, irresponsible tribunal, and the failure of the police to discover a clue would be explained by the secret sympathy of the inhabitants with the criminals. A very neat pamphlet would be published on the text to prove that the Irish people are a race of degraded assassins utterly unfit for self-government. How would the English people like the argument pressed home to themselves.

For those elements of the press determined to acquire Sir Charles Warren's scalp, the erasing of the Goulston Street writing was a godsend. The *Freeman's Journal*, who earlier if you remember had referred to Warren as having "strong and not altogether objectionable views," seemed to have changed their view of him at some point, possibly when it had appeared politically savvy to do so. On October 13th they described him in somewhat stronger terms:

He appears wholly incapable of doing anything but blunder from morning to night. He is now charged with having been the person who directed the writing on the wall over where the fragment of the apron was found in Colston [sic] street to be obliterated. The explanation offered by the police is that they feared an anti-Jewish outbreak in the East End. But it would have been quite easy for them to have had the writing covered, at least until it was photographed. Instead of that Sir Charles Warren instantly got all traces of it removed. This deserves to take rank as one of those blunders which is worse than a crime, for it amounts to this - that the chief of the London police destroys what seems to have been the most important clue yet obtained as to the identity of the murderer.

The *Cork Examiner* of October 11th were if anything even more vehement in their condemnation and managed to include Henry Matthews in the mix:

People in consequence are asking whether Warren is an imbecile or a criminal. Matthews, the Home Secretary, is of course primarily responsible, for as head of the Metropolitan police, he has systematically defended every act of Warren, no matter how absurd it may have been.

Matters were of course stirred up even further with the murder of Mary Kelly. Many newspapers predicted that Sir Charles Warren would have to resign, unaware that by that time he already had. The *Cork Examiner* of November 10th made the comparison to how such events would have been received in Ireland:

Little credit can be given to the police even should their efforts be crowned with success, which everyone must desire to see accomplished. The police have, it seems, commenced their old practice of refusing information to the Press, but it would not be at all surprising if it were ultimately through the agency of the Press and not of the police that the murderer were brought to justice. But it is a terrible state of things with which the inhabitants of London are confronted, and if the police fail in their duty, they and their leaders will suffer for it. In Ireland the police and their officers, and all the Removables and Incapables wax fat and strong as the popular indignation rises against them, but there is a striking difference in the circumstances of the police and the people in the two countries. It is, therefore, more than probable that Sir CHARLES WARREN and Mr MATTHEWS will have to go.

In truth, Warren was not at all the man he was made out to be. The accusations of his being a "military martinet" were in reality based simply on his attempts to modernise the force, and the accusation that he could not get along with his men seems to have been demonstrably fictitious, if the report of the *Times* of November 16th is anything to go by:

A deputation representing the whole of the Metropolitan Police Force waited on Sir Charles Warren at his private residence, St George's-road, yesterday, for the purpose of expressing their regret at his resignation.

Criticism of Matthews may have been somewhat more warranted. Indeed he was said to have been an unpopular man even within his own party, the general opinion being that he only retained his position on account of his Birmingham parliamentary seat being a marginal one such that the government could not afford to have him resign the whip. I will leave the last word however to the ever opinionated *Freeman's Journal*, and their final summation of the career of the departing Chief Commissioner:

> The administration of Sir Charles Warren has been marked with many serious failures. The curious tactics adopted by the London Police with regard to the right of public meeting in Trafalgar-square are yet fresh in the public mind. It may be remembered that in order to be logical Sir Charles Warren was compelled to discountenance any large demonstration in Trafalgar-square upon the occasion when the bronze statue of General Gordon was unveiled. Although the Government would gladly have used the opportunity offered for political capital, they were forced to adopt a course of action which resulted not in a mighty concourse moved to enthusiasm by the memory of the dead soldier, but in the secret meeting of about twenty officials, who unveiled the statue of the General, with little or none of that ceremony usually attendant on such occasions. Sir Charles Warren's attempt to subordinate the detective to the police force has been proven a ruinous experiment. To make the detective a policeman in plain clothes was his ambition. He succeeded so well that seven of the most brutal murders that have ever stained the records of a nation remain a mystery, unsolved and unpunished. So great an anxiety seems to have seized Sir Charles Warren to prevent the gathering of a London crowd that his officers actually caused to be obliterated the writing on the wall – the only evidence that Jack the Ripper left to mark in any way his inscrutable identity. Sir Charles Warren has been the victim of Mr. Matthews and of public opinion. It were idle for incapacity to seek to hold the reins of power for any considerable time, and we may confidently look forward to the speedy resignation too of Mr. Henry Matthews himself, ex Home Ruler, of Dungarvan fame.

SOURCES:

Paul Begg, *Jack the Ripper: The Definitive History*, Harlow: Pearson, 2003

Paul Begg & Keith Skinner, *The Scotland Yard Files*, London: Headline, 1992

Paul Begg, Martin Fido & Keith Skinner, *The Jack the Ripper A-Z*, London: Headline, 1996

Philip Bull, *Land, Politics & Nationalism*, Dublin: Gill & Macmillan, 1996

Christy Campbell, *Fenian Fire*, London: HarperCollins, 2002

Patricia Cornwell, *Portrait of a Killer: Jack the Ripper Case Closed*, London: Time Warner, 2003

Tom Cullen, *Autumn of Terror*, London: The Bodley Head, 1963

Stewart P Evans & Keith Skinner, T*he Ultimate Jack the Ripper Sourcebook*, London: Constable & Robinson, 2000

Donald McCormick, *The Identity of Jack the Ripper*, London: Jerrolds, 1959

Author's note: *In several of the newspaper reports reproduced I have corrected the inconsistent spelling of names. The majority of the reports reproduced here are from the collection I assembled during the research stage of my book but was unable to use in the final manuscript due to lack of space or due to repetition of ideas.*

Contemporary News Reports: Isn't That Interesting

By Wolf Vanderlinden

Wolf Vanderlinden is the Associate Editor of Ripper Notes.

In the past thirty years or so I have read a lot of newspaper reports concerning the Whitechapel murders. It is something that I enjoy doing because every now and then I come across something that makes me stop and say "Huh, isn't that interesting." (Now you know why this article has that stupid title. It's only marginally better than the original one: "Contemporary News Reports. Heaven Sent or Satan's Birdcage Liner".)

Reading contemporary news reports is not without its dangers, especially for those who are just starting out on the gruelling, twisting Whitechapel journey. Every once and a while you will end up wondering what ever happened to Mary Kelly's seven year old son or marvelling on how Mrs. Darrell, Mrs. Durrell and Mrs. Long all seemed to be passing Hanbury Street at exactly the same time in the early morning of the 8th of September, 1888, yet never saw each other. Both of these are examples of the pitfalls inherent in the newspaper study of the Whitechapel murders. But, as I said, every once in a while some article, or perhaps just a small part of an article, really catches the eye and forces you to throw caution to the wind and attempt to theorise based on this new snippet of information. The information may not be earth shattering or case breaking but merely intriguing. Perhaps the material can be looked at and interpreted a couple of different ways and might actually mean something. Or not. Here are three of these

interesting newspaper clippings as well as an explanation of why I have found them so fascinating.

Francis Tumblety

Mr. Tumblety Goes to Ottawa

In 1995 Stewart Evans and Paul Gainey published their important book *The Lodger, The Arrest & Escape of Jack the Ripper.*[1] In it they wrote of a newspaper report found in the *Montreal Commercial Advertiser,* 7 December, 1857, in which Ripper suspect Dr. Francis Tumblety claims that he had been asked to represent the Irish interests in the upcoming Colonial Parliamentary elections in opposition to Darcy McGee. This information was taken to be true, as it is in various other sources, including *The Jack the Ripper A-Z*,[2] several articles written about Tumblety and a city of Rochester historical website.

In fact this article actually appeared in several Montréal newspapers on the same day, which would seem to indicate that Tumblety really wanted to get the message out. Here is the article as found in the Evans and Gainey book:

> *As a candidate to represent the suffrages of the people of Montreal in opposition to Darcy McGee and that I am about to receive a most numerously signed address and I may add have resolved to come forward for the representation of the Irish interest. In allusion to the above statements, I may say it is not my intention at the present time to contest an election, but I have every hope, were I to do so, of ultimate success.*

Interesting stuff. Obviously the good doctor was so highly thought of by the Irish of Montréal that after only a few short months living amongst them he was deemed worthy enough to represent them in an election. An inestimable fellow, apparently, trustworthy and true.

Only one problem. It is highly unlikely that anyone asked Tumblety to run for office in this city against this man McGee in this election. It is not totally impossible but it is highly unlikely.

Now I don't want to deliver an in-depth lecture on Obscure Canadian Political History, fascinating as it may be, but some short background information is necessary.

The mass Irish migration to North America during and after the potato famine had lead to a swelling of the population of the city of Montréal so that by 1857 fully one third of the citizens were Irish. It was decided amongst the leaders of the Irish community that the Irish of Montréal were at a point where they needed two things: someone to write and edit their own newspaper — English in language; Irish in outlook and Roman Catholic in tenor — and someone to represent them in one of the city's three ridings in the Colonial Parliament. It was agreed that they could kill two birds with one stone if they asked Thomas D'arcy McGee to come to Canada East and fulfill both roles.

D'Arcy McGee had been an Irish revolutionary in his youth, a member of the Young Ireland movement, who had been forced to flee to the United States disguised as a priest. He had since become a newspaper reporter and editor; an author; poet; lecturer; historian; lawyer and passionate orator. He would go on to become a member of the Colonial Parliament; a Cabinet Minister; one of the most important and influential Fathers of Confederation (the founders of Canada); a member of the new Canadian Parliament and one of the greatest speakers that Canadian politics has ever seen. His support amongst the Irish citizens of Montréal in 1857 was almost total.

Tumblety had his good points too, of course. A man who knew him, Colonel C. S. Dunham, said of him *"A more arrant charlatan and quack never fattened on the hopes and fears of afflicted humanity."* As a political slogan this, perhaps, needs some work.

So what is the real message behind Tumblety's newspaper ads? Well, to me there seems three possibilities. The first is that, unlikely as it may seem, some disaffected portion of Montréal's Irish community did indeed ask Tumblety to run against McGee. The only fringe group, for that is what it would have had to have been, that was strongly opposed to McGee was the revolutionary Irish Nationalist movement.

After the failure of the Young Ireland

uprising of 1848 McGee had returned to his moderate political views, feeling that change for Ireland would only come through peaceful political means. This put him at odds with the more violent elements of Young Ireland. Men like James Stephens and John O'Mahony, who had been forced to flee to Paris, plotted the formation of a secret Irish revolutionary group which O'Mahony named the Fenian Brotherhood. These men saw D'Arcy McGee as soft and his moderate views as *"flatulent pablum."* Their anger increased when in 1855 McGee briefly returned to Ireland and lectured his countrymen against emigrating to America. He urged them to stay at home in order to maintain their religion, their language and culture but, he said, if they had to emigrate he suggested that Canada was a better environment for them than the slums of New York and Boston. Irish Americans were outraged. McGee was branded a traitor by the Fenians and their supporters, for how could any loyal Irishman claim that life under the Crown in British North America was preferable to life in the free United States?

Given this hatred[3] and the fact that there seems to have been some Fenian support in Montréal in later years it seems possible that Tumblety could have been asked by nascent elements of the Fenian movement in Canada to run against McGee. These Montréal newspaper ads, therefore, might be taken as evidence of Tumblety's Fenian leanings.

The second possibility is that these ads are merely another example of Tumblety's Barnum like showmanship and need for attention. Throughout his career the good "doctor" was able to put himself in the spotlight almost at will. Whether by riding through the streets mounted on a magnificent white stallion or driving an open carriage with matched pair or merely by parading around on foot dressed in some eccentric costume, usually followed by a dog or servant, Tumblety made sure that he was noticed. This flamboyancy seem to be part of Tumblety's character and it is not hard to see him as an extroverted flashy showman. The attention that he gained was also good for business especially if it got his name in the papers. The Montréal clippings thus might be an attempt to inject his name into the one topic that was on everybody's lips at the time: the Colonial Parliamentary elections. It should be noted that, as he turned down the supposed offer, Tumblety was able to become part of the political debate without actually having to do any politicking and without having to face the crushing defeat which he would surely have experienced. In a sense he could have his cake and eat it too.

The third, and perhaps most likely possibility, is that the answer lies in a mixture of both scenarios. Tumblety might not have been asked by anyone to run against D'Arcy McGee but as an Irish American he may have been one of those who harboured a grudge against the man. His announcements in all of the major Montréal newspapers would not only garner him some news copy but also allow him to tweak McGee's nose by claiming a numerously signed petition supporting his own candidacy in opposition to McGee's plus a declaration of ultimate success on election day had he in fact chosen to run.

From Hell, Mr. Byrnes

I found this next interesting piece while doing research on the Carrie Brown murder. It comes from the *New York Times*, 25 April, 1891.

...Inspector Byrnes apparently feels that the murderer must be arrested, for Inspector Byrnes has said that it

would be impossible for crimes such as "Jack the Ripper" committed in London to occur in New-York and the murderer not be found. He has not forgotten his words on the subject. He also remembers that he has a photographed letter, sent by a person who signed himself "Jack the Ripper," dated "Hell," and received eighteen months ago.

It is not the entire paragraph that I find interesting but merely the final sentence.

William Bryk, in his online article on Inspector Byrnes for the *New York Press*, has this to say about this passage:

In February or March, 1891, an interviewer asked Byrnes' opinion of the London police's handling of the Whitechapel murders: the savage mutilation of East End streetwalkers attributed to Jack the Ripper. The Chief Inspector commented that the London police had sent him a photograph of the Ripper's most famous letter, the signature boldly scrawled across the page, with its return address, 'From Hell.'

I have been unable so far to find the original mention of this letter in the *New York Times*, so I don't know in what context Byrnes received it, but I find it very interesting that Scotland Yard would send the Chief of the New York Detective Department a copy of what certainly must be the "Lusk letter." This letter, which was sent to Whitechapel Vigilance Committee head George Lusk, was accompanied by half a human kidney supposedly removed from the body of Catherine Eddowes.

It is possible that Byrnes had some suspect in custody or under surveillance whom he believed had some connection to the Ripper murders and thus wanted a sample of

The Lusk letter: a photograph of it was reportedly sent to investigators in Ne York.

the Whitechapel murderer's handwriting to compare with that of his suspect. This seems unlikely to me, however, and I can find no mention of any potential candidate from September to December, 1889, roughly around the date when Byrnes received the copy. Perhaps a likelier explanation is that Scotland Yard sent the copy of the letter as a gift to Byrnes, or potentially Inspector Walter Andrews sent it as a sort of thank you for aid given by Byrnes and his men when Dr. Tumblety had escaped to New York in December 1888. This question cannot be answered until more information is uncovered.

Two things, however, are interesting here. The first is that the sending of the "Lusk letter," rather than the "Dear Boss" letter or the "Saucy Jacky" postcard reiterates something that we already know: that several high ranking officials at Scotland Yard believed that the "Dear Boss" letter and the postcard were fakes.

Sir Charles Warren stated that *"the whole thing is a hoax."*[4] while Sir Robert Anderson, writing in *Blackwood's* magazine in 1910, stated that the "Jack the Ripper" letter *"is the creation of an enterprising London journalist."* Sir Melville Macnaghten said much the same thing. Chief Inspector Donald Swanson wrote in the margins of his copy of Anderson's autobiography that all head officers of the CID at Scotland Yard knew the identity of this journalist, while Chief Inspector Littlechild pointed the finger at either Thomas Bulling or John Moore, both of the Central News Agency.[5]

Interestingly this belief does not appear to have been unanimous. For one thing the "Dear Boss" letter was put on display in Scotland Yard's own Black Museum and identified to visitors as being from the killer. As well, when London police in October, 1896, received a letter signed "Jack the Ripper" replete with words and phrases from the "Dear Boss" letter they wondered if it could be genuine and proof that the killer had returned. Senior officers such as Detective Chief Inspector Henry Moore and, surprisingly, Chief Inspector Donald Swanson both looked into the matter and compared the 1896 letter with the original. Although both men felt that the two letters were not by the same individual it is interesting that they, especially Swanson, didn't offer the opinion that the original letter had been a journalistic hoax. Apparently the evidence that the "Dear Boss" letter had been written by a known journalist was not conclusive.

The second interesting observation is that someone at Scotland Yard apparently thought that the "Lusk letter" was actually genuine. Or, at least, possibly genuine enough to send a copy to an associate in America. The official word, however, seems to doubt the authenticity of the kidney sent with the note and thus doubt is obviously cast on the legitimacy of the letter as well.

That the kidney sent to George Lusk was a hoax seems clear if one trusts the words of the medical men who examined it, specifically those of Dr. Gordon Brown. Brown, who had performed the autopsy on the body of Eddowes, told a reporter from the *Sunday Times,* 21 October, 1888, that the kidney *"exhibits no trace of decomposition."* he also states that, although preserved in spirit (of wine, apparently), *"it has certainly not been in spirit for more than a week."* As Eddowes had been murdered September 30th it is impossible that her kidney could have been placed in preservative around the 13/14th of October without clear and obvious signs of decomposition. This, therefore, was not the kidney removed from Catherine Eddowes' body and, as a medical student's prank seems the likeliest conclusion, the "Lusk letter" is not genuine.

One of the few police officials who actually believed that the kidney was genuine was Major Henry Smith of the City Police. Perhaps, in the end, it was Smith and not someone from Scotland Yard who sent the copy of the letter to Byrnes. Either way the passage in the *New York Times* seems to indicate a belief on some unknown official's part that the "Lusk letter" was genuine and, by extension, the kidney sent with it.

Superintendant Arnold Speaks (Kind Of)

Superintendent Thomas Arnold was the head of H Division (Whitechapel) at the time of the Ripper murders. It was Arnold who asked permission from Sir Charles Warren to erase the Goulston Street graffito and it was also Arnold who arrived at Miller's Court to announce that the bloodhounds would not be coming and that the room should be entered. Arnold, therefore, was in the thick of the hunt for the Ripper and his opinions must be considered to be important – yet he apparently gave only one interview on the subject.

After his retirement from the force in 1893 Arnold was interviewed by the *Eastern Post*[6] and pretty much said that the Ripper murders were unsolved. It is also clear that he did not know the identity of the murderer nor did he have a suspect in mind. No suspect? From the head of H Division? What about the known police suspects like Druitt? Or Tumblety? Or Ostrog or Kosminski? An argument can obviously be made that Superintendent Arnold did not believe any of these men were the Ripper. I will now offer another interesting piece of evidence which seems to back this up.

When Carrie Brown's mutilated body was discovered in an East Side New York City flophouse American reporters immediately contacted Scotland Yard in order to gain their opinions on the matter. The *New York World* stated:

London, April 24. – Great interest is taken here in the news of the "Jack the Ripper" murder in New York. Scotland Yard received early advices of the tragedy, and it was quickly forwarded to the various chiefs of departments. The police authorities are inclined to think the absence of a gash in the throat of the New York victim indicates that the work is not that of the London "Ripper." Supt. Arnold states his belief that the original "Jack" is still in London."[7]

It is interesting that Superintendent Arnold states on the 24th of April, 1891, that he believes that the Ripper is still in London. This would thus exonerate Montague John Druitt who had committed suicide in December of 1888. It would also

rule out Dr. Francis Tumblety who had fled London on the 24th of November, 1888, and had never returned.

If we assume that Arnold was saying that the Ripper was still in London and *uncaught* then we can also rule out Michael Ostrog[8] who, although he was in London when Arnold spoke to the *World,* was sitting in a police cell waiting to be sentenced after his arrest on the 17th of April. We can also safely eliminate Aaron Kosminski for much the same reason.

Kosminski had been admitted to the Mile End Old Town Workhouse Infirmary on the 4th of February, 1891 and had been transferred to Colney Hatch Lunatic Asylum on February 7th. Interestingly if Aaron Kosminski was Sir Robert Anderson's Polish Jew suspect then his admittance to the asylum only weeks earlier seems to have made no impression on Superintendent Arnold or on the Scotland Yard officials who forwarded news of the Brown murder in New York to *"various chiefs of departments."*

The fact that Arnold believed in 1893 that the Ripper murders were unsolved and that the murderer was still possibly at large in London in 1891 has to put a new slant on the possible guilt or innocence of these four police suspects.

Isn't that interesting…

NOTES:

1. Century Publishing Ltd.

2. Begg, Paul; Fido, Martin; Skinner, Keith, *The Jack the Ripper A-Z,* Headline Book Publishing, 1991.

3. McGee would receive death threats for the rest of his short life. On the 7th of April, 1868, at 2:30 A.M., after a long session of Parliament, a Fenian supporter named Patrick James Whelan stepped up behind Thomas D'arcy

McGee as he attempted to place his key in the lock of his Ottawa boarding house. Whelan fired a single bullet into the back of McGee's neck, killing him almost instantly.

4. Letter to Godfrey Lushington 10 October.

5. Perhaps the earliest example of a finger being pointed at a newspaperman comes from George R. Sims, who wrote in the *Referee*, on 7 October, 1888: *"This proceeding on Jack's part betrays an inner knowledge of the news-paper world which is certainly surprising.*

Everything therefore points to the fact that the jokist is professionally connected with the Press."

6. 3 February, 1893

7. The *New York World* 25 April, 1891.

8. Ostrog is no longer a serious suspect. Phillip Sugden has proved that he had been arrested by the Paris police on 26 July, 1888, and was sentenced to two years in prison on 14 November. He was thus sitting in a French jail cell during the Whitechapel murders.

When the People Were in Terror

By Norman Hastings, with an introduction by Nicholas Connell

*The following series of articles by journalist **Norman Hastings**
was rediscovered by researcher **Nicholas Connell** a few years ago, but this
is the first time it has been reprinted. **Ripper Notes** would like to thank
Nicholas for transcribing the text and allowing it to be published here.*

The following account of the Whitechapel murders appeared in the London edition of the Dundee Saturday tabloid *Thomson's Weekly News*. It was published over an eight week period between September and November 1929. It was written in response to the book *The Mystery of Jack the Ripper* by Leonard Matters that had been published earlier that year. The author, Norman Hastings, was a frequent contributor to the newspaper through the 1920s and 1930s.

Hastings' assessment of the Borough poisoner George Chapman's viability as a Ripper suspect appeared in *Thomson's Weekly News* in June 1930 as part of a series of articles on Chapman's life and crimes. It too was written in response to a newly published book, *The Trial of George Chapman*, edited by H.L. Adam.

The newspaper text has been subject to some minor editing with corrections made to misspelled names of people and places.

-NC

Original introduction to the series:

Many readers will remember the days when Jack the Ripper walked the streets of London, and kept the population in a panic of terror. They may also recall how the terror spread, and it was rumoured that Jack the Ripper had been seen in many other cities. Since these dreadful days of 1888 interest in the mystery of Jack the Ripper has never ceased, and it has been revived lately by a new theory that Jack the Ripper was a doctor driven insane because of the ruin of his only son by a woman of the London streets. We now give the full story in a new form; this has been written by the famous criminologist, Norman Hastings, who has for long been collecting information regarding the doings of "The Terror."

Chapter One

On Easter Monday, in the year 1888, the silent Terror claimed his first woman victim in the East End of London, and within a few months, as crime succeeded crime, the whole country was thrown into a state of the wildest panic such as had never been known before. For Jack the Ripper–to give him the name by which he became afterwards known–had started his reign of terror.

Six years passed before his fiendish crimes ended as mysteriously as they had began, and those six years are stamped indelibly on the minds of all who passed through them.

To the womenfolk and children they were one long nightmare, when the coming darkness struck terror into their hearts lest this devil in human form should glide among them to carry on his fearful work of swift and silent murder and mutilation.

Even the bravest of men stood appalled at the revolting nature of each of the twelve crimes that were committed during this period, but the panic which seized the people was due even more to the uncanny manner in which Jack the Ripper went about his work.

Each of the twelve unfortunate women was done to death in a densely crowded area, where men were coming and going throughout the whole night, within a few feet of waking people, and where one cry for help would at once have brought a score of avengers on the trail of the Unknown.

But there was no cry. His victims died silently, and in a manner that was almost supernatural, Jack the Ripper glided away from his foul handwork, through the cordon of police and volunteers, and never once were his footsteps heard as he passed through the streets.

UNBELIEVABLE STATE OF TERROR

The knowledge that in their midst was a human devil who could pass noiselessly among them and murder at will was too much for the overwrought nerves of the women and children. As month succeeded month and Jack the Ripper was still at large and still planning fresh outrages that no human power seemed able to prevent, scenes of an extraordinary character took place all over the country.

Long before the end of the first year the East End of London was in an unbelievable state of terror. Three thousand women in the Whitechapel district alone fled from their homes to find peace of mind elsewhere. Those who were left dared not venture forth in the darkness alone. They went out only when they had to, in twos or threes, passing every dark alley with frightened haste, scared by the slightest shadow.

The panic communicated itself to the children. White faced and with staring eyes, they would run home from school imagining they were being pursued by Jack the Ripper.

At night, fathers, husbands and sons banded together to patrol the streets, to watch from darkened windows, cursing the stupidity of the police and vowing dreadful vengeance on the man who had brought terror into every household.

The East End of London swarmed with men in blue, with detectives in plain clothes and in innumerable disguises. With the assistance of women brave enough to offer their services, hundreds of traps were prepared for the Ripper. All in vain. With rage and horror in their souls, the citizens would greet the dawn only to learn that yet another woman had been savagely murdered within a few feet of safety.

The panic spread to the West End and the suburbs of London, and from thence to the provinces and to every remote village and hamlet in the kingdom. Every little community would be startled by the rumour that Jack the Ripper had found London too hot for him and had fled to their neighbourhood to continue his work. A terrified woman would come running home to say she had seen Jack the Ripper lurking in some dark lane, a knife in his hand and in his eyes a glare of madness. And if further proof was needed, she had seen him walk and had heard no sound.

That statement was enough. In a few hours the district would be in the wildest state of alarm. Search parties would be hurriedly organised, while women and children cowered in their homes until the danger had passed.

UGLY DEMONSTRATIONS

The feeling in London grew as the list of crimes increased and still the police were completely baffled by Jack the Ripper. There were ugly demonstrations everywhere.

Hundreds of suspects were detained and their lives placed in peril, for the enraged mobs were ready to carry out lynch law against anyone who was merely suspected of being connected with the crime.

The very suggestion that Jack the Ripper was a Jew was sufficient to stir up the bitterest racial feelings in the East End, and the most stringent precautions were necessary to prevent rioting.

A number of women, reduced to nervous wrecks by the terror around them, committed suicide. Practical jokers, of a brutal nature, took delight in pouncing on defenceless women in the dark and calling themselves "Jack the Ripper," until the effects of this class of crime grew so serious that the most severe punishment had to be introduced to check it.

Thousands of respectable homes were thrown into a state of fear by the receipt of bloodstained letters containing horrible threats and signed "Jack the Ripper."

There were even instances in the North of England of men who actually tried to imitate the work of the Terror. Each of these crimes, even though the murderer was discovered, added to the state of wild alarm into which the country had been thrown and which continued long after Jack the Ripper committed his last outrage in 1894. His identity had never been discovered, and it was felt that at any month he would reappear in London or in one of the provincial towns, and the periodical alarms continued.

The real extent of the terror of those days can be judged from the fact that as recently as 1911, a rumour that Jack the Ripper had been seen in North London was sufficient to send the whole metropolis into a state of fear. For weeks mothers waited outside the schoolgates to take their children home in safety – children who knew nothing of the crimes of 20 years before but who were terrified at the very mention of the name of Jack the Ripper.

Even today in the East End of London there are thousands to whom those years of dread can never be forgotten, and who shudder at the thought that perhaps Jack the Ripper is still alive and in their midst, and capable of one last crime.

SCENE OF FIRST OUTRAGE

At the time of Jack the Ripper's first outrage, no better district than Whitechapel could have been chosen by any murderer to carry out a series of crimes successfully.

The whole area east of Aldgate and Petticoat Lane, was one bewildering network of mean, narrow, silent, and darkened alleys and courts, their slum tenements and properties in the last stage of disrepair, and each one grossly overcrowded with families of every nationality. Jews and Cockneys were in the majority, but Germans, Russians, Poles and Asiatics made the strangest and most lawless community in London.

Except for the broad Whitechapel Road and Commercial Road the streets were badly lit by occasional gas-jets. The courts and alleys at night were in complete darkness, and lurking there could be found the scum of London, hiding from justice and secure in their retreats. Into most of the warrens the police never dared venture. The gangs of crooks and blackmailers who prowled the street at night were never molested.

Respectable citizens had protested in vain against the lawless condition of Whitechapel. Instead of cleaning up the district, the Chief Commissioner of Police, Sir Charles Warren, for some inexplicable reason, decided to change all the detectives in the East to duty in the West End and vice versa. Thus the very men who, by their local knowledge, could have first got on the trail of Jack the Ripper, were replaced by detectives who knew nothing about the inhabitants and knew not where to get the information that was so badly needed.

The fact that there were four police stations in this small area deterred no criminals, but there was one other drawback which they had to face. All through the night there would be unfortunate men and women drifting through the narrow streets, outcasts of society, who were apt to wander into the scene of some dark deed. And there were the workers at Spitalfields close by, always coming and going, who might prove dangerous witnesses. But bitter experience had taught them all to keep a discreet silence about what they chanced to see. It did not pay, in Whitechapel, to help the police too much.

Because of these two factors, inexperienced detectives and terrified witnesses, the first Whitechapel murder remained a complete mystery and its true significance was not realised until months had passed when it was too late to reopen the inquiry.

To those in authority it suggested nothing more than the cowardly work of a gang of ruffians. Little time was wasted in making investigation into the death of a woman, one of the unfortunates of the East End, whose friends and relatives were never traced. Emma Smith, the name by which she was known to women of her class, may not have been her true one, but adopted to hide her shame and some tragedy in her earlier life.

Forty years of age, of a quiet, secretive nature, she would never reveal to her acquaintances anything of her former life, beyond that she was a widow and had seen none of her former friends or relatives for over ten years. She had broken with them rather than they should know her shame. "They would not understand," she said on the only occasion she mentioned them, "but I must live somehow."

THE FIRST VICTIM

Easter Monday, 1888, came and found her living at a model lodging-house in Church Street, Spitalfields. The whole district was on holiday and throughout the day Emma Smith, remained indoors, but in the evening she dressed herself in her poor finery and made towards the Whitechapel High Road.

It was the rule at these lodging-houses that the women must return not later than 1 a.m. if they wished to keep their bed, but the time passed and there was no sign of the widow. Her companions paid no heed. She would turn up the next night.

At 4.30 a.m. the superintendent of the model was disturbed by a feeble rattling at the door.

"You're too late. There's no bed for you, whoever you are," he shouted out without bothering to go to the door.

The knocking, faint though it was, continued, and at length he stirred himself and went to give the caller a bit of his mind.

To his horror he found the form of a woman leaning against the step, and by the flickering light from the passage recognised the features of Emma Smith. She was covered in blood and had fallen into a

Down and Out! A woman of the class from which the Ripper took his victims.

swoon, but beyond that her face and ears were bleeding the man could see no serious injury.

He tried to rouse her but she was too far gone and without any more delay he whistled for the police.

When they arrived they made a quick examination of the woman and discovered that a terrible wound had been inflicted in the lower part of the body. There was no time to be lost. She was evidently bleeding to death and a cab was summoned to convey her to the London Hospital close at hand.

As the cab turned along Osborn Street into the Whitechapel Road, the woman opened her eyes and seemed to recognise where she was. She signalled to the police officers and pointed out into the street to Whitechapel Church but a few yards away.

"There" she managed to say, and the cab was stopped. She was trying to tell the police where the crime had been committed, and sure enough on the pavement outside the church they saw the marks of blood, and the trail of the wounded woman as she dragged herself home.

Eagerly they questioned her as to what had happened.

"They were following me and I tried to get away. I crossed the street but they caught me."

She was asked to describe her assailants but only replied that "he was a young man."

The police asked her about the others, but she shook her head as if she did not understand and after saying the attack occurred at half-past one, she relapsed into unconsciousness. From this she did not recover and died twenty-four hours later in the hospital, leaving the police in a confused state as to what had occurred.

From the first they were of the opinion that Emma Smith had been attacked and robbed by a gang of ruffians whose path she had crossed, and as no money was found in her purse, the motive to them was clear.

CORONER FAR FROM SATISFIED

That the unfortunate woman had been stabbed in a barbarous fashion and that the robbery could have been committed without going to such an awful extreme, did not cause them any anxiety.

They tried to find witnesses but failed, although it is scarcely possible that someone did not see the victim during the three hours she took to drag herself a matter of three hundred yards to safety.

The opinion of the police was that of the public. Emma Smith had fallen in with the dreaded gang of blackmailers in the district and resisting their demands, had paid the penalty. There was no use trying to help the police in such a matter, otherwise the gang would soon have their revenge.

The movements of the ringleaders of the gang on the night of the murder were made the subject of examination, without any result. Nor could the relatives of Emma Smith be found, and the case was dropped as quickly as possible.

At the inquest proceedings the Coroner showed that he was far from satisfied about the affair. The nature of the wounds on the victim, such as may have been made by a blunt knife used with tremendous force and the real lack of motive for such a crime, together with the conflicting statement of the woman as to whether she had been the victim of one man or a gang, made him express uneasiness at the possibility of some particularly brutal murderer being at large in the district.

A verdict of wilful murder by some person or persons unknown was returned and Whitechapel, except for treating the blackmailers with even more respect than ever, promptly forgot all about the affair.

Life went on just the same as usual in the East End. The lawless element laughed at the power of the police, who, in their efforts to regain some measure of control, were given long beats which they had to patrol every forty minutes or so. Their movements could be timed to a nicety, and the unknown Terror, whose presence had not yet been suspected by anyone, could wait and plan his next outrage, knowing well the time he would have at his disposal.

THE SECOND OUTRAGE

His opportunity came on the night of August 7, a Bank Holiday. Within twenty-four hours the whole of London was speculating as to the identity of the murderer, while criminal classes of the East End seemed to sense that among their number was now one more deadly, more purposeful, more cunning than them all.

As in the first case, the victim was a woman of the unfortunate class, while her injuries were even more barbarous than those inflicted on Emma Smith. Less than one hundred yards from where the latter met her fate, the body of Martha Turner was discovered in the early hours of the morning.

George Yard Buildings, just off Commercial Street, had once been a weaving factory, and had been converted into flats which housed many families.

Every night at eleven, the caretaker turned out the few gas jets lighting up the landings and that Bank Holiday night, most of the families returning late had to make their way cautiously up the stairs to reach their rooms.

The last couple, Mr and Mrs Mahoney, reached home shortly before two o'clock. They came up the stairs together without noticing anything unusual. A quarter of an hour later Mrs Mahoney came down again to buy some fish and chips for her supper, and even on her return she saw nothing suspicious.

Her footsteps died away and for an hour the silence over the building remained undisturbed, until the return of yet another of its residents. Albert Crow, a cabman, who had been reaping a rich harvest that day, and when he climbed the stairs he was tired out and eager for his bed.

He had reached the first landing when suddenly he stood still. Lying there, outstretched and on her back, was the form of a woman just visible in the growing dawn. The cabby gave one glance, and then stepping over the form, made his way to his flat.

"Another drunk," he muttered to himself. "She may as well stay as she is." Such a sight was common in the district, and the cabby was one of those men who prefer to steer clear of trouble of any kind.

A WOMAN'S PREMONITION

He went to his bed and forgot all about the incident, but Mrs Reeves, the wife of a docker, who lived next door to him on the same floor, could find no peace that night. Several times she had awakened her husband to tell him that she was sure there had been something dreadful going on below. Her husband laughed at her fears, thinking her mind was taken up with the usual holiday rows that had been going on the previous evening.

But he could not reassure her, and when he left for his work shortly before five o'clock in the morning she repeated her fears.

He went down the stairs laughing at her nervousness, but what he saw on the first landing, drove the blood from his cheeks, and sent him running off for a policeman. P.C. Barrett came quickly to the spot, but one glimpse of the poor woman there unnerved him and fully a minute passed before he could steady himself enough to make a proper examination.

The woman was lying on her back on the stone floor in a pool of blood, her clothing disarranged, her hands tightly clenched as in agony, and her body mutilated in a fearful fashion. The two men could not speak. They stood appalled at the awful sight.

Detectives were summoned at once, while another constable ran for Dr Kileen, who practised among the poor of Brick Lane. He answered the call immediately, and was the first to realise the full significance of the methods of the unknown murderer whose nickname was soon to throw the whole country into a state of panic.

No fewer than thirty-nine wounds were discovered on the body, and of those the majority had been inflicted after death, with a small knife skilfully used.

Nothing like it had ever been known before, and though the police tried to keep their discoveries secret until the body had been identified, yet the news passed swiftly round and a tremendous crowd gathered outside George Yard Buildings.

There was no difficulty in identification. Martha Turner had been well known, and though her features had been disfigured, yet a number of her companions recognised her and gave her address as 4 Star Place.

Almost at once on inquiry into her movements on the previous day, the police made a discovery which seemed helpful, but which, in truth, led them away from the unknown murderer.

Martha Turner had spent the evening with Mary Connolly, the latter well known as Pearly Poll, and at eleven o'clock they had met two soldiers. Shortly before midnight Pearly Poll and her male companion left Martha Turner and her soldier outside the entrance to George Yard Buildings, and Martha Turner had never again been seen alive.

Pearly Poll was at once taken to the Tower of London where the soldiers were paraded before her, but she failed to identify the two men who had accosted her and her companion.

The police felt convinced that they were on the right track. The soldier must have brutally murdered the woman with his bayonet for some reason unguessed at. They ignored the fact that Mrs Mahoney had not tripped over the body at half-past two in the morning, where it would certainly have been lying if the murder had been committed by the soldier about midnight. In addition, between twelve and one there had been a dozen residents, some with lights, who had made their way up the stairs and not one of them had seen anything suspicious or heard any cries.

It followed that the murder in all probability, took place between 2.30 and 3.30 a.m., but the police stuck obstinately to their own theory. They made house to house searches in the neighbourhood for any deserters, while as the time passed, and still they made no progress, the public indignation made itself heard.

The ordinary public were certain there was some connection between the latest outrage and the murder of Emma Smith, but they believed both crimes to have been committed by the gang of blackmailers known as the "High Rip" gang who were terrorising the whole district. The very name

This archway led to the scene of one of Jack the Ripper's early murders.

of the gang was suggestive. Crowds gathered to demonstrate against the police. Indignation meetings were held. Women began to stay in at nights in case they would be the next to be murdered.

And then was heard for the first time the whisper that one man alone was guilty. Where it originated no one ever found out, but it spread quickly through the ranks of the criminal class. They spoke fearfully of the "Ripper" who was out to kill as many women as he could.

The police scoffed at the rumour, but they quickly found that there were others who believed it. While making their inquiries after the two wanted soldiers, they met with refusals to give any information whatever on the grounds that the Ripper would murder any informer.

Pearly Poll heard this talk and disappeared. She was terrified. Her evidence would be essential at the Coroner's inquest, but she was afraid to speak. For days the police hunted her in vain, and then she was found in hiding in Covent Garden. She persisted in her statement about the soldiers, and that day when taken to the barracks at Chelsea, she deliberately picked out the first two soldiers she saw, although they could not possibly have been connected with the crime.

Little headway was made in the case. The husband of Martha Turner, a furniture packer, called Samuel Tabram, of Greenwich, told how his wife had left him nine years previously and associated with another man whose name she took. She was a woman who had no enemies, and as far as could be discovered there was no reason whatever why she should have been the victim of such a crime.

THE RIPPER STRIKES AGAIN

The usual formal verdict was returned of murder against some person unknown, but in response to the public outcry detectives were drafted in from Scotland Yard to help in the case. The unusual features of the murder had impressed themselves on the minds of all the East End. Martha Turner had undoubtedly been murdered at the spot where her body was found.

The Unknown had done his work in silence and had got clear away. Somewhere close at hand he was in hiding, waiting his chance to strike again. This conviction grew stronger and stronger despite the inspired official statements. Detectives worked day and night after the closing of the inquest on Martha Turner to get on the track of the Unknown.

Messages were published stating that they were on the verge of success. The murderer in his hiding place must have been amused at the futile efforts of the police. A week passed. Success was as far off as ever and then, as though determined to end all argument and place his existence beyond all doubt, Jack the Ripper struck again. On the morning of September 1, the country awoke to the real horror of the crimes that were only just beginning.

It was the crowded area round Buck's Row, off Brady Street, that the police had been combing in search of suspects who had worn the Queen's uniform and for the black-mailing gang, and it was by Buck's Row that Jack the Ripper left evidence of his handwork which was to startle the whole world.

At half-past three in the morning Charles Cross, a middle-aged carman, made his way down Buck's Row to start his day's work. He was whistling as he went, and was passing the stable of the Essex Wharf when in the yellow light of a flickering gas jet, he caught sight of a woman lying huddled up in the gateway. She was lying in the shadow, her head almost touching the gate which stood back three or four yards from the pavement.

Although he was in a hurry to get to his

work, and this was apparently but a case of a woman in a drunken slumber, his curiosity got the better of him and he crossed the road to where she was lying.

Her bonnet was by her side. Her head was curiously twisted but the carman never guessed the reason. He took her hand and shook her. She never stirred. Her clothing was disarranged.

As he explained afterwards – and his statement throws much light on the conditions then prevailing in the East End – he thought it was a woman who had been assaulted and outraged and had fallen into a swoon. He had no more time to waste so he started for his work again determined to inform any policeman of the discovery should he happen to meet one.

Instead, he had gone but a few yards when he was approached by a stranger, also dressed like a carman, who turned away from him as though he feared an attack.

"Come and look here," Cross cried out reassuringly; "here's a woman been knocked about."

The stranger came across the road. There was nothing suspicious about his manner and he and Cross together examined the form lying stretched out. Her hands were very cold. The stranger felt her heart.

"I think she's breathing," he said. "But it's very little, if she is."

"Right-o, I'll tell the police," Cross replied and they parted, the stranger never being heard of again, and neither of them realising the full extent of the crime which had been committed.

REAL TRUTH BEHIND
THE MURDER

Cross did not meet a policeman until he was almost at his work and before then, P.C. Neil making his regular beat, had passed along Buck's Row and shone his lantern on the figure lying so still. The light from the bull's-eye revealed that which the two carmen had missed. Her head was almost severed from her body.

The shrill blasts of his whistle brought other officers to his side and within a few minutes Dr Llewellyn, whose surgery was in the Whitechapel Road, hurried round and pronounced life extinct. She had been done to death within the previous hour and the wound in the throat meant instant death.

There was no need for him to make further examination and he hurried back to his bed, while the police, after arranging for the body to be taken to the mortuary, made inquiries at the houses and from the night watchmen around.

They were baffled from the beginning. Everyone was prepared to swear they had heard no one passing along the street except the two carmen. No murder could possibly have been committed there.

They were still pursuing their inquiries when at the mortuary a discovery was made which revealed the real truth behind the murder to the somewhat indifferent police and stirred them into instant action.

Dr Llewellyn was summoned to the mortuary. He was surprised at the urgency of the call but he understood when he saw the body of the unfortunate woman. The wound in the throat had been made from right to left suggesting a left-handed assailant, but it was the other wounds that mattered.

Three sharp, ferocious incisions had been made in the lower part of the body with the deftness and the certainty of a surgeon. The unfortunate woman had been mutilated with a definite object in view and all done coolly on the pavement, with discovery possible at any moment.

No longer was there any doubt as to the existence of Jack the Ripper. Messages for assistance were sent at once to Scotland Yard. Every officer was sent to the scene of the crime to carry out the investigations.

A hurried conference of the chiefs was held, and they decided to withhold the revolting details of this fresh crime, but it was too late. The news passed from lip to lip with astonishing rapidity. Long before midday the streets about Buck's Row and the police station were packed with the assembled crowds, who spoke in undertones about Jack the Ripper and angrily demanded better police protection.

When night fell the crowds rapidly dispersed. Women barricaded themselves in their houses, and watched from their windows to get a glimpse of any suspect. They knew they would never hear him. Outside the patrols kept their watch. Over the whole of the East End brooded a tense feeling of further impending disaster.

Jack the Ripper was at large. The six years of terror had begun.

Chapter Two

The panic that seized hold of the East End of London immediately following the discovery of the terrible crime in Buck's Row was instinctive. The people sensed, long before the police, that in their midst was a slayer of women, whose work would not cease until he had been caught.

Official messages of reassurance were put out that day in vain. As soon as darkness fell extraordinary scenes took place all over Whitechapel and Mile End. Women rushed to their homes to lock themselves in and keep guard over their children. All night long tradesmen were kept employed making the dwelling houses secure. Feeble lamps were hung up in the numerous courts and alleys, to aid the first volunteer patrols who kept watch until the dawn.

Women of the unfortunate class were in a pitiful state of alarm. They could not appeal to the police for protection. They were defenceless and almost entirely at the mercy of the Terror once he had marked them down. Hundreds of them left their haunts in the overcrowded lodging-houses with which Whitechapel was full, and made their way to other, and safer districts.

Few slept that night. Those who went to bed lay awake trying to catch the sound of a furtive footfall that would tell them the Terror had passed them by. They were convinced the police would never catch him.

Despite their optimistic statements, the detectives engaged on the case were baffled by the Buck's Row murder, and what they did discover only served to increase the general alarm.

No difficulty was experienced in identifying the poor woman whose throat had been cut, and whose body had been mutilated. Her companions recognised her as Mary Ann Nichols, aged 38, who had shared a tiny room in a lodging-house at 18 Thrawl Street, Spitalfields. The women had separate beds, for which they paid 4d. a night. In the lodging-house were over 70 other women.

She had been out all day, but on her return at midnight had confessed she had no money to pay for her bed.

"I'll soon get my doss money," she said as she made off, but turned back to show her friends her hat. "See what a jolly bonnet I've got now," she remarked proudly. That was the bonnet that was found three hours later lying beside her mangled body in the darkened gateway in Buck's Row.

At half-past two she had been seen standing at the spot in Osborn Street where the first victim of the unknown murderer had met her death, 500 yards from Buck's Row, where the constable found her a little over an hour later.

BAFFLED POLICE

That was the whole information the police could get about her movements that night. They were baffled. At first they declared the murder could never have been committed in Buck's Row. Little blood had been found at the spot, but they had come across a faint red trail running along Brady Street, showing how the murderer had carried his victim along, twice crossing the road in the course of 150 yards before he noticed the gateway.

None of the people who lived about could throw any light on the mystery. Mrs Green, lying awake ten yards away, had heard nothing. Two watchmen on the Essex Wharf no further away, had been on the alert all night and were prepared to swear that not a soul had passed that way except the constable on his beat.

This uncanny element in the crime was strengthened by a remarkable story told by Mrs Colwell, of Brady Street, along which the Terror was believed to have passed with his burden.

"I was awakened shortly after three," she said, "when I heard a woman calling out 'Murder, murder,' and then 'Oh, don't, don't.' I heard her run away and further down the street there was the sound of a scuffle, and blows being struck. Her cries got weaker and weaker, and then she must have turned into Buck's Row. I lay in bed, shivering with fright and unable to move, for though I heard her footsteps plainly, yet I never made out the slightest sound made by the man who was chasing her and doing her to death."

This account of the silent Terror passed swiftly around and caused the greatest consternation, backed as it was by the evidence of Mrs Green and the two watchmen. The police thought Mrs Colwell's story a highly exaggerated one, but it fitted in with the common idea of the unknown murderer, who was putting every home into a state of fear.

"LEATHER APRON"

He was looked upon as being almost a phantom. The police had not the slightest clue to his identity, but soon there was a whisper that he could be none other than Leather Apron, a man who prowled the streets at midnight, bullying and maltreating women, and because of the rubber soles on his shoes, moved about in absolute silence.

No other man but he was capable of the awful murders that had taken place. Extraordinary instances of his brutality were told. The cry, "Lynch Leather Apron" was taken up on every side, and search parties were organised to get on his track before he could break out again.

A short, thick-set man of Jewish appearance, badly clad, with a long black moustache and small glittering eyes, he had earned his nickname because of the small leather apron he invariably wore when prowling the streets after dark. No one seemed to know his real name. He was believed to be the head of the "High Rip" gang of blackmailers, and beyond doubt was a man of the most vicious type whose name had been a byword in the East End for years. When it was discovered that he had disappeared on the night Martha Turner met her death in George Yard Buildings, the public needed no further evidence of his guilt, and the demand for his arrest was overwhelming.

The police made a few enquiries, and they, too, became infected by the popular feeling. On the second night after the Buck's Row murder a description of Leather Apron – name unknown – was circulated all over the country, as it was believed he had made his way to the provinces.

In the East End this news was hailed with joy and relief, but it spread the panic to every city in the kingdom. Leather Apron was among them! From all parts came word that the wanted man had been seen lurking about the countryside, waiting for another victim!

Two days of terror followed until the statement was made that Leather Apron had been seen back in Whitechapel, and his arrest was a matter of certainty. A further 24 hours went by with still no word of his capture. The people, enraged beyond measure at the thought that their prey would escape them, formed a procession to march in protest to the West End. Before they reached the City they were met by the police and dispersed.

AN UNFORTUNATE INCIDENT

An incident that occurred while they were returning home shows how deep was the popular feeling at this period. Several hundred of the men were passing through Commercial Road when the cry went up that Leather Apron and one of his gang had been arrested in the street.

A few moments later six constables were seen forcing their way through the crowds, gripping two frightened looking men, one of whom wore a leather apron. The mob did not stop to ask questions.

"Here's Leather Apron and one of his gang. Let's lynch 'em, boys."

The cry was taken up. From every little street scores of men came running at the call, and in a trice the constables were in the middle of a wild surging mob, striving desperately to reach the two prisoners. Batons were drawn, police whistles were blown, and from the police station constables came pouring to help quell the riot. The fight continued desperately for five minutes until over a hundred police had been rushed to the scene and the angry crowd forced back.

Another attempt to capture the two men – now scared to death, and protesting their innocence – was made, before they reached the shelter of the police station. Even then the trouble had not finished. Barricades had to be erected or the station would have been stormed there and then. The situation had become very ugly, when the station superintendent had a notice pinned up outside, which announced that the two men in custody were slaughtermen, who had nothing whatever to do with Leather Apron, but who had been taken in charge for their own safety, as their identity had been first mistaken by some women.

The crowd, realising their folly, melted away, but this scene was repeated three times in different parts of the East End that night.

Next day Leather Apron, alias John Pizer, was found in hiding in a house in Mulberry Street, by a detective who had been keeping watch continuously for forty-eight hours. Forewarned by the events the previous evening, the detective allowed Leather Apron to walk beside him in a normal manner until they reached Leman Street Police Station. Leather Apron was well aware of his danger and was only too glad to join in the ruse.

Really he should have been taken to Commercial Street Station but that was far too risky. As it was, no sooner was Leather Apron under lock and key than the crowd got wind of his arrest, and within a half-hour 10,000 people were clamouring outside and police reinforcements had to be summoned from the East End. The mob knew that Leather Apron would have to be transferred, and they were waiting their chance, but again they were cheated for the suspect was taken away at three a.m.

LEATHER APRON CLEARS HIMSELF

The news that he had been laid by the heels had an immediate effect all over the country. Women went to bed confident that the Terror could no longer frighten them, and for the first time since the murder of Mary Nichols, the East End went back to its usual life.

Had they known the truth, they would never have slept so peacefully, but the police were beginning to learn wisdom. Leather Apron had made a detailed statement as to his movements during the previous ten days, a statement that was corroborated in every particular. He should have been liberated at once, but the temper of the mob being what it was, such a step would have been sheer folly. Leather Apron, himself, refused to leave his cell, and it was finally arranged that he should be detained until the resumed inquest on Mrs Nichols. There he would be able to clear himself, and in the meantime the people would remain calm, thinking the guilty man had been caught.

Once again the inquest was held at the Working Lads' Institute, with Mr Wynne Baxter as the Coroner, the court being almost entirely filled with detectives, while a strong posse of police were on guard outside.

Police witnesses confessed that they could make nothing of the case. Mrs Nichols had been lured to Buck's Row after the constable had passed the spot on his beat, and the crime committed before he returned there half an hour later.

The terrible mutilations had been inflicted while she was fully clothed, but no one had seen the murderer making his escape, nor had any weapon been found. Every lodging-house had been searched, whole streets combed but no suspect had been heard of.

Leather Apron's innocence was completely established.

Mr Smith, the father of the murdered woman, broke down when he told how he had recognised his girl only by a childhood mark on her forehead. She had been separated from her husband for seven years following a quarrel over a nurse, and sinking lower and lower had been forced to enter the workhouse at Lambeth. Latterly her father had lost all trace of her, and only after she was murdered did he know the kind of life she had finally led.

JURYMAN'S OUTBURST

Pity for her, and those of her kind, led to an impassioned outburst by the foreman of the jury in bringing in the usual verdict of murdered by some person unknown.

"Why don't the police offer a reward?" he demanded. "Had Mrs Nichols been a rich woman living in the West End, they would have offered £1000. But she is a poor unfortunate, and so they take no notice. These women have souls just like other women, and I myself will offer £25 to anybody who can tell me anything which will help."

His words were echoed everywhere. Prominent merchants in the City combined to offer a £500 reward, while the poor of Whitechapel had a house to house collection now that the inquest had revealed to them the truth that the Terror was still at large.

The police were at their wits' end, when word came to them of the arrest of a suspect in Gravesend to which the greatest importance was attached. Word was broadcast everywhere to try and allay the disquiet, and at first it certainly seemed as if the captured man, William Piggott, a middle-aged docker, had been concerned in the Whitechapel outrages.

THE RIPPER IS BUSY AGAIN

But somewhere in the neighbourhood Jack the Ripper was still lurking, unknown, unheard, unseen. As if mocking the police and to scatter their theories to the winds, that night he once more came from his hiding place, and by his most sensational crime up till then, proved the innocence of William Piggott, and threw London into a greater state of panic than ever.

Through the ring of police and patrolmen he passed in the daylight, and in a little backyard in Hanbury Street, where he could have been caught like a rat in a trap, he silently murdered Annie Chapman, and his cruel work over, with the marks of his crime still on him, made his way unseen to safety.

No sooner had he gone than the body was discovered, and the hue and cry was put up, but Jack the Ripper had vanished as if into thin air. His victim, another poor, defenceless walker of the streets, had assisted in her own doom when she consented to enter that little yard.

Hanbury Street, along which the funeral cortege of Mary Nichols had passed the day before, consisted almost entirely of dwelling houses of a mean and sordid type, in which families of every nationality lived.

Seventeen persons lived in one of the buildings which had one common door, kept open day and night. From this door to the back of the house was a long dark passage leading into a small yard, some 15 feet square, and separated from the adjoining yards by a four foot fence. In the centre, a rickety stair led to the underground cellar and workshop used by Mrs Richardson.

Two months before burglars had passed through the passage, just swung open the door at the farther end, and had stolen a number of tools from the cellar. From that time, her son John, a porter at Spitalfields, had made a habit of looking in at the yard on his way to work to make sure that all was well.

On the night of September 7 Mrs Richardson slept very poorly, being kept awake by the sudden and intense cold. She heard her son arrive and make his way to the yard.

John Richardson pushed the back door open, saw the cellar door was undisturbed, and having a few minutes to spare sat down on the two steps leading from the passage to the yard, and repaired one of his boots. At five o'clock he got up and made his way to the market, and in the growing daylight had seen nothing suspicious.

At 20 minutes past five, Mrs Long passing along Hanbury Street, saw a woman standing talking outside No. 29 to a dark, foreign man, wearing a brown deer stalker hat, but she paid no particular attention.

"Will you?" she heard the man say. "Yes" replied the woman, and they made their way into the passage.

A minute or two later Albert Cadosch who lived next door, got up and went down to his yard to get some water. While there he overheard a couple talking in the yard of 29.

"No, no," he distinctly heard a woman saying. Then there was the sound of a slight scuffle and all was quiet. By merely looking over the low fence he would have been bound to see what was going on, but Cadosch just turned and went back to his room.

It was left to John Davis, a labourer, who lived with his wife and three children at the top of No. 29, to make the discovery.

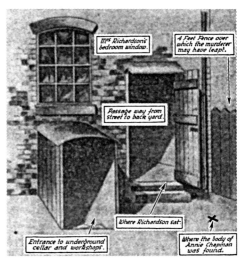

Scene of backyard where the body of Annie Chapman was found.

Rising at quarter to six, he made a cup of tea for himself and Mrs Davis.

"I'm going down for a breath of fresh air," he told his wife. It was broad daylight by then and he walked quickly along the passage, pushed open the swing door and stepped down.

What he saw drove him running into the street shouting "murder," and calling for help. Two men came up just as he collapsed on the pavement.

"There's a woman dead in there," he said, pointing to the passage. "She's – she's – I can't face it again."

The two men hurried in. They knew already who had been at work, but the sight that met their eyes was too much for them.

Just to the left of the steps, her head against the fence, lay Annie Chapman. Her head had been almost severed, and a coloured handkerchief was tied tightly round it, as if to keep it in position. As in the case of Mary Nichols, the clothing had been disarranged, and the body shockingly mutilated. At her feet lay her few personal possessions neatly arranged.

No time was wasted before the police were called to the spot and every available officer set to work making investigations. Dr Phillips, the divisional surgeon, came along within a quarter of an hour to report that without doubt the mutilations were the same as those carried out on the body of Mary Nichols.

The chin had been forced back while two deep wounds were inflicted on the throat. The three incisions on the body had been made with the deftness and skill of a surgeon's hand, and Dr Phillips confessed that he himself could not have done it in the short time available to the murderer. One part of the body had been carried away, and the guilty man had not even stopped to clean his hands or clothing at the tap in the yard. He could easily have placed the body down the steps leading to the cellar, but instead he left it for the first caller to discover.

While this examination was going on, Mrs Richardson, roused from her sleep, sent her little grandson down to find out what was wrong. He saw the body, and with his little face white with terror, ran shrieking up the stairs. "Oh, granny, there's a woman been murdered. The Ripper has come! The Ripper has come!" His mind had been so worked up by the prevailing fear that even he knew who had committed the crime.

VICTIM'S ONCE HAPPY DAYS

Details of the unfortunate woman were more easily got. Annie Chapman had seen better days, when she lived happily with her family at Windsor. Four years previously she had parted from her husband – a head coachman – and coming to the East End had associated with a sievemaker. When he left her, she used her needle to earn a living, selling antimacassars and crochet work at Stratford Market.

Nine months before her death, at the age of 44, and when her husband no longer sent her money, poverty had driven her on to the streets, and she had become one of the unfortunates, who lived together at a Dorset Street lodging-house.

One valuable piece of information was gathered at the lodging-house. She had been in the habit of wearing two rings made of brass on her finger and these, it was discovered had been torn away by the murderer, who possibly thought they were valuable.

A watch was kept on every pawn-broker's shop in London as the only hope of finding the Unknown, for there was not one other clue which would aid in his capture. Once again Jack the Ripper had outwitted the police, and knowing the situation the public fear grew and grew.

One woman in Kensington who had been frightened by an encounter with a man in the dark whom she believed to be the Ripper, fell dead from shock on reading of the Hanbury Street outrage.

THE WRITING ON THE WALL

In another passage in the street was found chalked up the following message: "This is the fourth. I will murder sixteen more and then give myself up," – and in their unreasoning fear, the people believed the message to be a true one.

A tremendous crowd gathered at the scene of the latest murder, and they would not be shifted. From the windows of neighbouring houses, they were able to catch a glimpse of the yard at 29 and see the packing cases thrown there, which still could not conceal the track of blood. Householders charged the morbid sightseers a penny each for this privilege.

The patrols were strengthened at night. Every device was adopted to lure the murderer into a trap. Wild suggestions were made as to the identity of the murderer, but the publication of the fact that the murderer had taken away one part of the body brought a promising clue from a well known hospital doctor.

He stated that he had recently been approached by a rich American who wished to obtain certain anatomical specimens for his own experiments and was prepared to pay heavily for them. He hoped to get them from paupers who died in hospital, as it was necessary they should be obtained from women who had just died. On finding the hospital authorities could not help him he had gone off without giving his real name and saying he would have to try elsewhere.

Immediately the public believed that the Ripper would not rest until he had satisfied the demands of the American and that there would be many more murders to be recorded. At once there was an exodus from the East End of frightened women, few of whom ever returned to their homes.

To add to the general panic, a few days after the Annie Chapman murder, a similar crime was committed near Gateshead-on-Tyne where Jane Beetmore was found in a ditch at Birkley Hall, lying murdered and mutilated. At last the Whitechapel murderer had found a new area for his activities.

Dr Phillips and Scotland Yard men travelled north, and the circumstances were so identical that at first they thought it was the work of the same man. Scenes which had occurred in the East End were repeated in the industrial districts of the north, and the panic spread across the border, where it was reported that the fugitive had gone on to Scotland.

Ultimately the crime was brought home to the young woman's sweetheart, who had merely imitated the Whitechapel Terror, but until that was established the whole of the north was in a ferment.

London had gone crazy with fear. Their tempers worn fine by loss of sleep, the people were ready to riot against the police at the slightest excuse. Women who were employed at night in the tailors shops and in the markets would not venture out unless under police protection. Children were afraid to go to school. False reports of further murders were common every night and drove the people to their homes, leaving the streets deserted and shopkeepers in dismay.

All kinds of private rewards were offered for information. Stockbrokers in the City clubbed together for a £1000 reward, but nobody knew or had seen the Unknown.

THE RIPPER'S BOAST

The inquest on Annie Chapman had come to an end without any further valuable information having been obtained, when a London newsagency received a blood smeared postcard with an East End postal mark and penned in red ink.

It ran: -

Dear Boss,

I keep on hearing the police have caught me, but they won't fix me yet. I have laughed when they look so clever and talk about being on the right track. Great joke about Leather Apron. Gave me real fits. I am down on women, and I shan't "give up" ripping until I get buckled. Grand job the last was. I gave the lady no time to squeal. How can they catch me? I love my work, and want to start again. You will soon hear of me again with my funny little games. Ha! Ha! The next job I shall do I shall clip the lady's ears and send to the police. Keep this letter back until I do another job, and then send it out straight.

(signed) Jack the Ripper.

From that day the silent Terror became known as Jack the Ripper. The very mention of the nickname struck fear into the hearts of the people. They waited in dread for his next move, wondering who amongst them would be his victim.

Police recruits were hastily drafted into the East End. The patrols were doubled but three days later on the night of September 30, Jack the Ripper came again from his hiding place, and eluding the watchers eclipsed all his previous crimes.

Disturbed while at his work on his first victim, he slipped away into the darkness to strike down yet another woman. His purpose completed he passed safely through the ring of watchers unseen and unheard.

Chapter Three

Until Sunday, September 30, 1888, the people still believed that Jack the Ripper would be caught. Let the police here take proper measures to safeguard the district and the murderer would not long escape vengeance.

The events of that night left them in despair. Every possible precaution had been taken. The anonymous letter with its threat of further atrocities had put the police on their guard. The streets were kept under constant patrol. No corner was left unvisited for more than fifteen minutes. Usually ten minutes saw the constable back again. All suspicious characters were stopped and questioned. In addition, there were the volunteer patrols.

But as if mocking at all their efforts, Jack the Ripper stole into the streets once more. Within an hour two women had been murdered by his hand. Each time he was within an ace of capture, but in a miraculous manner made his escape, unseen and unheard.

Surprised while about to begin work on the motionless body of his first victim in Berner Street he vanished into the shadows, thwarted for the time being, but relentless in his purpose.

Five minutes later the hue and cry was up, and acting on a pre-arranged plan a cordon was drawn round the whole district by the sound of the first alarm. Jack the Ripper passed through them somehow and, in less than an hour, the second body had been found in Aldgate. Mitre Square was left unguarded for fourteen minutes, but in that short time he carried out his purpose, leaving behind a body mutilated worse even than any of the others.

His reply to the special measures taken by the police, left the people convinced that Jack the Ripper would never be caught. Nothing could stop him. They could only wonder when and where the next blow would fall. It was a terrible period of suspense.

Apart from the terror they caused, each of the crimes was attended by a number of singular circumstances which kept the public interest in them at a high pitch.

THE BERNER STREET MYSTERY

The anonymous postcard from Jack the Ripper with its threat, had been kept a secret, and the folk who lived in Berner Street never dreamed he would come near them that night. At one time the street had been known as Tigers' Bay, it being the refuge of the most desperate criminals in London, but the police had cleaned it out and now it was comparatively a respectable street in which to live.

Half-way along was one dark, narrow court, leading out to the Commercial Road. At the entrance were two large wooden gates, in one of which was a small wicket gate for use of the residents when the larger gates were closed. This was but seldom used and on this Saturday night, because of the large number of folk coming and going, nobody bothered to lock up.

No more than 12 feet wide, the whole length of the court on the right was taken up by the rear of a social club with a back entrance into the court. On the left-hand side ran a dead wall for five or six yards and then a number of cottages.

There were no lamps, and after sunset the court was shrouded in absolute darkness. The light from the windows of the social club falling on the upper part of the cottages opposite served to emphasise the general gloom. Yet it was a very unlikely place for Jack the Ripper to visit, for men and women were constantly going in and out of the club which was one of the most successful and best conducted in the East End.

Known as the International Working Men's Educational Club, its members consisted almost entirely of Russians, Germans, Poles, and Continental Jews and that evening well-known speakers had come to lecture them on the progress of socialism in Germany. By 8.30 over two hundred men and women were in the small hall, and the debate went on till 11, while outside the rain was falling heavily.

It cleared up at that time and by half past 11, 30 or 40 members were left in the hall. They formed the choir, and as usual, they began to sing songs of the homeland with a genuine sense of music and to the enjoyment of the folk living opposite.

At half-past 12, to hear them better, Mrs Mortimer came to the gate of her cottage at

Mrs Mortimer suddenly became aware of a man hurrying along the opposite side of the street carrying a shiny black bag. She had not heard his footsteps, and did not hear him even then.

No. 36. A few minutes later she saw the chairman of the club, Mr Eagle, make his way in after escorting one of the lady members home. The singing went on and then she saw another member come out into the court and stroll up and down, evidently just to get a breath of fresh air.

He stayed for five minutes and then the court was again deserted. For ten minutes Mrs Mortimer remained at her gate and she saw no one enter the court nor did she hear anything suspicious. She was just about to enter her home when in the distance she could make out the sound of a pony and cart, which she at once guessed to be that of Mr Diemschutz, the steward of the club, who regularly every Saturday night went out to the market with drapery goods, returning about one in the morning.

At the same instant she was suddenly aware of a man about 30, dressed in black and carrying a small, shiny black bag, hurrying along the opposite side of the road, as though he had just come in by the gate. Mrs Mortimer was a little startled, for she had not heard his footsteps, nor could she hear him even then.

He walked quickly, turning his head

away from her and vanishing round the corner making towards Commercial Road.

Mrs Mortimer made her way indoors, the choir opposite singing some Russian melody. No sooner had her door closed to than the pony and cart reached the gates leading into the court. The steward had returned. He was feeling tired and glad to get home. The pony had quickened its step to pass through the familiar gateway, but suddenly and unaccountably pulled up and shied back.

The steward urged it on but the pony refused to budge. Mr Diemschutz was naturally pulling it towards the right to make for the club entrance but when at length it did move, the pony persisted in making for the left wall against which it pulled up.

The driver was puzzled. Never had the pony behaved in such a strange manner before and at last he concluded that there must be some obstacle in the court which he could not see in the darkness. He stood up and looked round. There was nothing in front, but to the right he saw a mass, almost against the wall.

"It's mud," he said to himself. "But how did it get here?"

To satisfy himself he leaned over and prodded at it with the handle of his whip, to find that he had struck something hard. The explanation of the pony's conduct came to him instinctively. Before he got out of the cart he knew that it was the body of a woman lying there. With shaking hands he struck a match and his worst fears were confirmed.

Without troubling to make an examination he turned and ran towards the club entrance six yards away. A few seconds later the singing inside stopped abruptly, and then the steward came out with another man – the only one bold enough to make an examination.

In the candlelight they stooped over the body hoping against hope that it was simply a drunk woman. She was lying on her left side, face downwards, as if she had fallen forwards, her head in the little gutter which ran close to the wall. Her head had been almost severed in one cut.

In a few seconds the court was filled with the excited, gesticulating foreigners, who scarcely knew what to do until the steward roused them by ordering them to fetch the police.

Once more Dr Phillips was summoned. He found the body quite warm. The woman was dressed quite poorly in black, her check silk scarf wound lightly round her neck. In her right hand she was still grasping a little bag containing cachous, while pinned on her dress was a faded rose. Dark complexioned with curling hair, her features were sharp and pinched and her obvious poverty showed that this had been no crime of robbery.

DISTURBED AT WORK

There were none of the characteristic mutilations of Jack the Ripper. It was evident he had been disturbed by the arrival of the steward and had made his escape in the nick of time.

The victim's right hand and arm were covered in blood. Her clothes were all muddy as though she had been dragged along the ground a little. Dr Phillips, taking careful notes was able to piece together what had happened.

Entering the court, the murderer had seized hold of his victim and grasping the scarf round her neck had attempted to cut her throat. She had struggled violently before he was able to accomplish his object, and the position of her clothing told eloquently of what he was about to do when he had been alarmed by the sudden arrival of the steward and took to flight.

While this examination was going on the police were acting with the greatest promptitude.

The club members were detained and each man compelled to make a full statement of his movements. Over in the cottages the people were roused and the valuable evidence of Mrs Mortimer obtained which showed what a narrow escape Jack the Ripper had had.

Alarmed by the activity of the police, the people were soon up and about trying to find out what was wrong, but it was some time before they learned that the murder had taken place in the court in Berner Street, which had been hurriedly barricaded at both ends to keep away the crowds.

By half-past one, three hundred police were engaged in the hunt for the murderer while eight minute's walk from Berner

Street, Jack the Ripper, heedless of his danger, was carrying out his second crime that night.

The news of that murder came as a bombshell to the police. The circumstances of the crime seemed incredible.

Mitre Square stands just inside the City of London boundary at the back of St Katherine Cree Church. Almost forty yards square, it was overlooked on three sides by large warehouses, while on the fourth side were two dwelling houses, one empty and the other occupied by a policeman who had gone to bed at midnight after a long spell of duty on the look out for Jack the Ripper.

Unlike most of the squares in the Whitechapel area it was comparatively well lit. A main carriage-way led into Aldgate High Street, while on the opposite side were two smaller courts, one leading to the orange market in Houndsditch.

By midnight the neighbourhood was the centre of activity. The small traders were all making their preparations for the opening of the market in Petticoat Lane on the Sunday morning, and people were in the habit of taking the short cut through the square from Petticoat Lane into the City.

P.C. Watkins, a conscientious and reliable officer, was on patrol in that area and he was timed to pass through Mitre Square every fourteen minutes. At half-past one precisely he looked in. All was quiet.

He was about to depart when he was hailed by George Morris, the watchman, at one of the warehouses.

"Did you 'ear the whistles up Whitechapel way just now?" he asked. The constable nodded.

"Sounds to me like Jack the Ripper again," the watchman said, "I only 'ope he comes 'ere. I've been waiting for 'im all week."

THE NIGHT'S SECOND TRAGEDY

P.C. Watkins wished him luck and passed on. He had heard nothing definite of the Berner Street murder up till then, but passers-by acquainted him with the rumours and this put him on the alert. Promptly at sixteen minutes to two he turned back into the court. All seemed well when his eye caught a dim outline against the wall near the carriage-way entrance.

He shone his lantern and uttered a cry of horror. Rapidly he walked over, made a quick examination and was almost stunned by what he saw. A few seconds later he was battering at the door of the warehouse where the watchman was on guard.

"For God's sake, mate, come to my assistance," he called.

"Hold on till I get my lantern," Morris called back. When they were together, he noticed the constable was on the point of collapse.

"Oh, dear," he said. "Here's another woman been cut to pieces."

"Where?"

Watkins pointed to the corner. Without any delay, the watchman pulled out his whistle and the alarm was sounded, and the City Police took control.

It was their first experience of Jack the Ripper and they had to deal with a case even more gruesome than any of the others.

A shabbily dressed woman of fine physique, she had been left lying on her back with limbs extended. Her throat had been cut, her body mutilated while in addition her features had been deliberately disfigured. The lower eyelids had been nicked away, a slash across the face had removed part of the nose while half the right ear was missing, to be found later among the victim's clothes.

Detective Halse, who was present at the medical examination, first grasped the significance of this. He remembered the anonymous postcard sent by Jack the Ripper in which he wrote ".... The next job I shall do I shall clip the lady's ears and send them to the police."

This threat had never been made public, so the murderer must be the man who made that threat.

Two other clues were found. Lying near the body were three small boot-buttons, whereas the woman wore lace-up boots, while part of her dark apron had been cut away and removed as if to carry the parts of the body that were missing.

A CRYPTIC MESSAGE

The City Police were quickly organised to deal with the search, but their work was hampered by the rapidly growing crowds which collected round the square. The people poured out in their tens of thousands, armed with knives and pokers with some vague idea of catching the Ripper, though their coming made the escape of the murderer a certainty.

Hampered and harassed at every turn, the City Police yet came across the clue they were looking for. At three o'clock in the morning P.C. Long, while patrolling along Goulston Street, looked up the staircase of a model lodging-house, at 108, and there he found the missing part of the apron, covered in blood where the murderer had wiped his hands and clothing.

He did not dare to give the alarm nor leave the spot in case Jack the Ripper was in that house. While waiting for any other officer to pass along he made a careful inspection of the place and on a wall nearby came across a cryptic message written in chalk.

It ran:-

"The Jewes are the men who will not be blamed for nothing."

The constable had passed that spot half an hour before and neither the apron nor the writing on the wall were there then, so they must have been placed there by the murderer.

At last another officer came by. Word was sent to the detectives and Detective Halse, recognising the importance of the clue, placed men on guard at the spot with orders that the writing was to be photographed as soon after daylight as possible.

This clue was destroyed by the order of Sir Charles Warren, the Chief Commissioner of Police, who soon after arrived. Without consulting anyone he had it rubbed out on the ground that it would create a terrible riot later in the day once the people got to know of it. Probably he was right in believing that there would have been trouble but his action brought severe criticism when it was made public many days afterwards.

His whole concern was to try and calm the district. Military reinforcements were provided for in case that Sunday should see a riot as a result of the panic which would spread at the news.

But though London was in a state of intense excitement and fear, yet contrary to expectation, there was little trouble. All day long the streets were blocked with morbid sightseers, but the residents remained indoors overcome with gloomy despair, wondering who among them would be the next to die at the hands of Jack the Ripper.

The wife of a silk weaver in Hanbury Street, haunted by fear, hanged herself that morning when she heard the news and was found dead by her eight -year-old daughter. Two other women took poison and were removed to hospital in a serious condition.

VICTIM'S IDENTITY

The extraordinary thing was that the two cases were dealt with by different branches of the police and they made little attempt at co-operating.

The City Police were the more successful in their inquiries that day and identified the Mitre Square victim as Catherine Eddowes, aged 43, who, strangely enough, had been in custody at Bishopsgate Police Station until one o'clock that morning.

She had just returned from hop-picking with a man, and while he went to a model lodging-house, she left him to seek shelter at the casual ward. She managed to get some boots to pawn and at ten o'clock on the Saturday night was taken in charge by a constable and kept locked up until "she was able to take care of herself."

At one o'clock the gaoler was sure she was quite well. In fact he hadn't noticed much wrong with her at all, so he unlocked the cell.

"This way, missus," he said, "pass along the passage and don't forget to shut the door."

"All right, good-night old sport," she

replied and made off towards Hounsditch to be almost immediately intercepted by Jack the Ripper and done to death.

At first the dead woman was believed to be Elizabeth Stride, aged 37, who was a Swede and had married a carpenter. After the death of her husband she had lived at Dorset Street with a man who positively identified her, as did a number of other women.

Little was known of her history except that she had lost her husband and two children who had been drowned in the Princess Alice disaster in the Thames.

On the Sunday evening, however, the police had a visitor, A Mrs M---- [sic] who was in tears and begged to see the body at the mortuary. On viewing it she went into hysterics and said it was that of her sister who had married the son of a wealthy Bath spirit merchant. She had been discovered in a guilty friendship with one of the servants and had been driven from home with her two children. In the five years that followed she had to live in shame but Mrs M---- had struggled to give her every assistance.

Each Saturday afternoon her sister met her at Chancery Lane and was handed two shillings from the hard-earned money of Mrs M----. She never said where she was living except that it was somewhere in Whitechapel nor in five years had she ever missed an appointment.

The previous Saturday she had failed to turn up, and at one o'clock, the time of the discovery of the crime in Berner Street, Mrs M---- had a vivid dream in which her sister kissed her three times.

Mrs M---- identified the body by what she described as an adder bite on the leg, and by various other circumstances. She repeated her sad story in court in a very convincing manner and the Coroner for a fortnight was puzzled by this question of identity until it was found that Mrs M---- was telling nothing but a pack of lies with the object of giving her sister, who was alive, a bad name.

Quite apart from this, the police by Sunday night had established that the woman, whoever she was, had been seen in the company of a man of 30, dressed in black and carrying some kind of parcel, a few minutes before the crime was discovered.

On Monday morning another surprise was waiting the detectives. Another postcard was received from Jack the Ripper of a startling nature.

It ran:-

I was not codding, dear old boss, when I gave you the tip. You'll hear about Saucy Jack's work to-morrow. Double event this time. No. 1 squealed a bit. Couldn't finish straight off. Had not time to get ears for the police. Thanks for keeping letter back till I got to work again.

Jack the Ripper

This was sent to a news agency and had been posted early on the Sunday, at a time when actual details of the two murders were being kept strictly secret. Indeed, pressmen had the utmost difficulty in getting any information about them and were quite unaware that the ear of Catherine Eddowes had been severed.

Opinion was sharply divided as to whether the postcards were genuine or a hoax, but in the light of all that happened, it seems certain that the writer knew only what the murderer could be expected to tell.

At first it was thought that Jack the Ripper must first drug the women in some way or another, and in response to the public clamour, a special examination of the bodies of Elizabeth Stride and Catherine Eddowes was made. Neither drugs nor narcotics had been used.

Hundreds of other suggestions were made. Bloodhounds were brought from Yorkshire and tried out by Sir Charles Warren on Tooting Common. They failed dismally.

TERROR SPREADS OVER COUNTRY

Amid the general horror there was not lacking humorous incidents. One detective shadowed a suspect in Bow all night long, captured his man after a long struggle, and discovered at the police station that he was a Scotland Yard plain clothes man. Another detective followed a man into a taxi yard in King's Cross, and while keeping observation from inside a cab, was set upon by the cleaners and stabbed for being a burglar.

In Newcastle the stabbing of a girl by a young man was enough to cause a stampede in the shopping centres. Women and children were injured in the rush to escape from Jack the Ripper.

Five women held a seance at Cardiff, and predicted he would come there the following week, and the townsfolk waited in terror of his coming. He had been seen entering a wood near Croydon after each crime and armed volunteers were stationed in the district to protect the womenfolk and make a thorough search.

Disturbances were caused in Govan, Plymouth and Bromley by false alarms. Tramps were chased away from most of the farms. Indeed the lonely districts felt the terror most, for women there had to go about unprotected. But the most remarkable incident of all occurred in Liverpool. Near the end of October a strong rumour got abroad that Jack the Ripper was a sailor, who celebrated each shore leave by a murder. For some strange reason all were agreed that he had left London, and that Liverpool would be his next port of call. It was useless trying to convince the people otherwise.

The patrols actually gave up their work in the East End of London while in Liverpool preparations were made to deal with the menace. Not to be outdone by the men, the women who lived there by the docks, clamoured for and were given long knives to carry about with them for their protection.

Scotland had its share of excitement and fear. In Edinburgh the hue and cry for a suspect was started. He was pursued to Glasgow but made his way to Greenock and then to Belfast before he was caught. There was no real ground for suspicion against him but he had fled because of fear of what would happen to him if the people laid hands on him.

So the weeks passed by with everyone wondering when Jack the Ripper would be heard of again. Further police precautions had been taken, but no one had faith in them. Extra gas lamps had been hurriedly fitted into most of the dark alleys and courts to thwart the murderer. Once again he did the unexpected and in her own home Jack the Ripper took toll of his next victim.

Chapter Four

The panic which had spread to the provinces following the double murder in Berner Street and Mitre Square, showed no sign of dying away quickly. Nothing could shake the popular belief that Jack the Ripper intended to leave the East End of London to carry out his work elsewhere.

The West End alone had remained undisturbed. Its well-to-do residents were not at all concerned by the fate of the unfortunate women on the other side of the city. They saw to it that their own streets were properly lit and patrolled, and that was the end of the matter.

But less than a month after the double crime, Mayfair was jolted out of its feeling of security.

On November 1, a party of workmen were finishing their labours for the day at the site of the new police headquarters in Whitehall – where Scotland Yard now stands. Some old buildings had been pulled down and one of the workers was passing through the vaults when he noticed a parcel lying among the masonry.

It was tied up tightly and the workman in his hurry to get home, bothered no more about it other than to report the find to the foreman. The latter was busy, and the parcel was forgotten until the following afternoon when one of the carpenters was sent down to the vaults to investigate.

He had to strike a match to see properly. He tried to lift the parcel but it was very heavy while the smell from it was becoming overpowering. Without breaking it open he went back to the foreman and a labourer was sent along.

A TERRIBLE DISCOVERY

On cutting the string round the wrapping of dark material, he was horrified to find the trunk of a woman's body, the limbs and head being missing.

There was no delay this time in getting police help. A dozen detectives were soon across from Scotland Yard and at once they jumped to the conclusion that this was a fresh atrocity on the part of Jack the Ripper, and a determined effort was made to hush up the affair.

The woman had met her death at least six weeks previously, but Dr Bond, who made the examination found nothing which would indicate the manner in which it was done, although in all probability her throat had been cut before she had been dismembered. About twenty-five years of age, of mature build, the part of the black-roche silk dress in which the trunk had been tied, showed that she belonged to a better class of people. One of the organs of the body was missing – a characteristic of the Jack the Ripper murders.

It was recalled that five weeks before, the arm of a woman had been found at low tide in the mud above Grosvenor Road Bridge over the Thames. This was found to fit perfectly into the right shoulder of the trunk, while the left arm was later found under some debris on the Whitehall site. The hands were well cared for, and showed no sign of household work.

News of the discovery soon leaked out, and the West End heard it with dismay. Jack the Ripper had come among them and they were to share the horrors of the East End.

TRYING TO SET THE MINDS
OF THE PEOPLE AT REST

At the hastily summoned inquest, an attempt was made to set the minds of the people at rest by pointing out that the Whitehall discovery was not likely to be the work of the Whitechapel murderer, as such pains had been taken to hide the body, whereas Jack the Ripper left his victims to be found by the first passer-by.

It was no use. Public opinion fastened on the fact that part of the body was missing, and that the dismemberment had been carried out with considerable skill. That was proof enough.

Without voicing their secret fear, the best known families in Mayfair retired to their country residences for a month or more. Questions were asked in Parliament about the danger to which the wealthy were being exposed, and by a score of such signs it was evident that the West End was every bit as scared as other parts of the country.

Only by solving the Whitehall mystery, and showing that it was not the work of Jack the Ripper, could the police hope to quiet

the general fear, but this they were never able to do.

The identity of the woman victim was never made known, though the cases of hundreds of missing women were investigated. Not a single clue was found as to where she met her death or the manner in which it was done, nor were the head and missing limbs ever discovered.

The records of Scotland Yard show how complete was the failure of the police in this affair, which, in their opinion, however, was not likely to be the work of the Whitechapel murderer. No matter what the experts thought, its effect on the people was very marked. They were quite sure it was the beginning of a new campaign on the part of Jack the Ripper, and bitter demands were made for the resignation of Sir Charles Warren, the Chief Commissioner of Police.

A WELCOME RELIEF

At the height of the controversy, the coming of the Lord Mayor's Show brought welcome relief to everybody. Forty years on it was regarded as a wonderful sight, and the procession through the City, with its blaze of pageantry, and the brilliant display of gorgeous uniforms, made an irresistible appeal to Londoners.

Among those who had looked forward to seeing the show was Marie Jeanette Kelly, who lived alone in a single room at No. 13 Miller's Court, Dorset Street, Whitechapel.

Twenty-three years of age, and of prepossessing appearance, her life had been an unhappy one. Jack the Ripper and his deeds had filled her with terror, and on the night before the Lord Mayor's Show she had given way to tears of regret, and said she was going back to her mother in Wales just as soon as ever she could.

"This will be the last time I shall see the show," she said to Lizzie Albrook, a girl of nineteen. "Then I will go back home. Don't you do wrong, Lizzie, as I did, or you will turn out just like me."

Morning came, but Marie Kelly was not among the carefree throng which made its way towards the City. She was sleeping her last long sleep in her little room, a victim of

Jack the Ripper. There was no longer need to argue where he had gone.

SUDDEN SILENCE THAT FELL ON THE CROWD

At mid-day the cheering and the enthusiasm in the City was at its height when the hoarse cries of the newsboys came as a bombshell. Those who were present that day will never forget the sudden silence that fell over the crowd, a silence that was not even broken when the Lord Mayor rode past.

The morbid minded streamed, in their tens of thousands, to Whitechapel, but when they reached Dorset Street they found their way barred by huge barricades which had been hastily erected, and which prevented even residents from reaching their homes.

Inside the little room the doctors were engaged in the awful task of collecting together the remains of Marie Kelly. During the night Jack the Ripper had plenty of time in which to carry on his work, which in this instance could only be that of a madman.

It was the first time he had committed murder indoors. Everybody in Miller's Court knew the unfortunate girl, and the police at last had hopes that they would get enough information to lead them to the unknown Terror. Information they got in plenty, but of such a contradictory nature as to leave them completely baffled, and which stamps the Miller's Court crime as the most puzzling of all the Whitechapel murders.

Dorset Street, off which the court runs, contained practically nothing but warehouses and lodging-houses, which had accommodated no fewer than fifteen hundred persons and were generally well filled. The street was brilliantly lighted and at any time of the day or night, there would be scores of people loitering about.

Miller's Court itself was approached by an arched passage, three feet wide and unlighted, from which opened two doors, leading to the houses on either side, which had a frontage on Dorset Street. The house on the left was kept as a chandler's shop by John McCarthy, while Marie Kelly had her room on the ground floor of the house on the right.

COUPLE SEEMED FOND OF ONE ANOTHER

Very little was known about Marie Kelly except that she had come from Ireland, and had had a very hard life.

Ten months before she had rented room No. 13, John McCarthy, the chandler, being her landlord. For most of the time she had been friendly with a young man, Joseph Barnett, and the couple had seemed very fond of one another.

Latterly he had taken exception to her generosity in allowing one of the unfortunates to take shelter in the house on occasions, and they had separated on the Tuesday, two days before the murder. Although the rent was many weeks in arrears, McCarthy, the landlord, had allowed her to continue occupying the room.

At eight o'clock on the Thursday evening, Joseph Barnett had paid a friendly call on her and promised to send her some money to help pay off the rent.

Marie Kelly had drawn his attention to a bill which had been posted up outside her window offering a £100 reward for information about Jack the Ripper, of whom she stood in great fear, in common with the other women in the neighbourhood.

She was rather despondent that evening and when she met Lizzie Albrook a few minutes after Barnett had gone, she broke down in tears. She remained in her room for two hours until her tears gave way to recklessness. An hour later one or two neighbours noticed that she had been out drinking – an unusual occurrence with her.

At midnight, Mary Cox, a middle-aged woman, who lived at No. 5 Miller's Court, and knew the girl very well, ran into her in Dorset Street. She was walking towards her home in company with a short stout man, shabbily dressed with a longish coat and a hard black billycock hat, who was carrying a pot of ale in his hand.

"I'M GOING IN TO HAVE A SONG"

She followed the couple through the passage and, as Marie Kelly was about to enter her room, she called out, "I'm going in to have a song," while the man seemed impatient at the interruption, and got her inside as soon as he could.

Early the next morning John McCarthy

opened up his shop, and fully expected Marie Kelly to come in for a few purchases before nine as was her custom. He meant to challenge her about the rent arrears.

There was no sign of her, and at a quarter to ten he sent his handyman, Thomas Bowyer, along to see if she had slipped away. Bowyer knocked at the door, but there was no response. He tried the handle. It was locked.

This was something he could not understand, so he made his way out into the court so that he might see through one of the windows if she were in the room. One of the windows was broken, and he put his hand in, pulled aside the curtain, and peered in.

He stepped back in horror, and almost at once ran for McCarthy. "What's the matter, man?" the latter asked.

"Governor, I knocked at the door," stammered the man with fright, "but I couldn't make her answer. I looked through the window and saw a lot of blood. She's been all cut up."

"Good God, do you mean to say that's happened?" McCarthy replied. Unable to believe the truth, he went and looked through the window himself, and a second later Bowyer was running for the police with strict orders not to tell anybody on the way.

The inspector came round from Commercial Street Police Station, and a call was put through to Scotland Yard. Unfortunately at this point there had been a misunderstanding over instructions regarding the use of bloodhounds.

Sir Charles Warren had ordered that the next time a body was found it was not to be disturbed in any way until the two bloodhounds he had been testing had arrived on the scene and could pick up the scent before any examination was made.

For two hours the police waited outside the room, while the barricades were being thrown up at each end of Dorset Street, and the occupants of the lodging-houses compelled to keep to their rooms. At the end of that time it was learned that the owner of the bloodhounds, fearful lest his dogs would be poisoned by the Ripper, had had them sent back to Scarborough.

It was practically mid-day when at length the door of the room was forced open by a pick-axe, and the detectives and doctors were able to state that no part of the body was missing from the room

It was the work of a madman. Even the face had been badly disfigured, as though a senseless attempt had been made to render identification difficult. Senseless because even the murderer must have known that everyone would be able to identify her in her own home.

The doctors were of the opinion that death had occurred at least six hours before, but there was one circumstance which made their task difficult. On entering the room everyone had remarked how stifling was the atmosphere in spite of the broken window, which should have let in the fresh air.

There was no fire in the grate, but the kettle standing there had been melted at the spout, indicating that there had been a big blaze there. The candles, which had been used to light the rooms, had been burned right down.

The girl's clothing had practically all gone while it was found that other clothing which should have been in the house was also missing.

From these facts the detectives reconstructed the crime.

Marie Kelly had been offered some exceptional inducement by the stranger in the billycock hat, and had allowed him to come to her home. There she had sat singing for over an hour while Jack the Ripper calmly contemplated another murder.

He had brought home the ale with him rather than visit a public-house in her company, and so give the police a clue to his identity.

Some time in the night he had murdered her in her sleep, but the candles gave out, and to have sufficient light for his purpose, he had to burn all her clothing he could find in the grate, and the heat had been enough to partly melt the kettle. Then he had left the room, locking it behind him, and walked off with the key.

Mary Cox was able to give a fairly detailed description of the man, and this was circulated at once, and there were good reasons to believe that Jack the Ripper would at last be run to earth.

These conclusions were reached within three or four hours, and the remains were placed in a coffin to be removed to the mortuary.

The horror caused throughout the

country by this latest crime, can be easily imagined, but there was no outbreak due to panic. The optimism of the police was infectious. Scores of arrests were made, and the people expected any minute to hear that the right man had been caught.

Unknown to the public, however, the police had been confronted by evidence which they simply could not understand.

Caroline Maxwell, a woman with a good reputation, whose husband was deputy at 14 Dorset Street, next to Miller's Court, was emphatic that she had seen Marie Kelly two hours before her body was found in room 13.

Mrs Maxwell said that at eight o'clock on Friday morning, she was just going to the chandler's shop, when she saw the girl Kelly standing in the passage leading to the court. She looked very ill and the elder woman went over to ask her what was wrong.

"I feel so bad," she replied, "I was drinking last night, and it's made me ill."

She asked what she could take to make her better and after a few more words, Mrs Maxwell left her and presumed she went indoors.

The circumstantial account of her meeting with the girl she told at the inquest, and refused to be shaken on any point.

WALKING WITH
A WELL-DRESSED MAN

In addition to this, a young man, George Hutchinson, came forward, who said that he had seen her at 2 a.m. on the Friday morning in Dorset Street. She had been drinking and told him that she must have money for the morning.

Hutchinson was well acquainted with her, and she left him and he saw her a minute or two later walking towards her home with a very well-dressed man. He wore a felt hat with a long, dark astrakhan coat, and dark spats. From his appearance with his moustache turned up at each end, he was a foreigner with a good deal of money.

Both Mrs Maxwell and Hutchinson were dependable, but their statements upset all the calculations of the police. The girl Kelly might very well have met a second man that night, but the doctors were definite that she could not have been alive at eight in the morning although they had to confess they had been unable to state with any degree of certainty when the murder had taken place.

The police were perplexed. They tried every avenue of inquiry, but only managed to get some details of the victim's earlier life. She had been brought up in Ireland, and then her parents had removed to Carmarthenshire, in Wales.

Eventually she reached the West End of London, finally taking up her abode in Whitechapel.

CONFESSION OF FAILURE

At every turn the police were up against a blank wall, and the people realised that once again Jack the Ripper was to go free. Their patience reached a limit when the following confession of failure was posted up outside every police station:

MURDER
PARDON

Whereas on November 8th or 9th, in Miller's Court, Dorset Street, Spitalfields, Marie Jeanette Kelly, was murdered by some person or persons unknown, the Secretary of State will advise the granting of Her Majesty's pardon to any accomplice (not being a person who contrived, or actually committed the murder) who shall give such information as shall lead to the discovery and conviction of the person or persons who committed the murder.

(signed)
Charles Warren.

This offer, coming after the refusal to allow any official monetary rewards to be made in connection with the crimes, at once caused an outcry. The people understood that the police were powerless to deal with Jack the Ripper. Fear took hold of them and anger too.

The storm of indignation was so great that a few days later the resignation of Sir Charles Warren was suddenly announced, and a successor was sought who could deal with the menace in the East End, and quieten the whole country.

No headway was ever made with the Miller's Court murder, and the panic was growing steadily, when a thick fog enveloped London for four days. Few women dared to go into the streets. It was an ideal opportunity for Jack the Ripper, but the time passed without further crime.

This led to the theory that Jack the Ripper was not a Londoner at all, but lived in the provinces and paid periodical visits to Whitechapel which he must have known pretty well some years before.

Scotland Yard were of the opinion that the man might belong to Manchester, basing this on reports they had received of a suspect who had several times made his way back there the morning after a murder. Guards were asked to keep a look out, while six detectives kept watch at the London stations for two months without success.

Many readers will no doubt remember the consternation that was caused in Manchester when news of this leaked out, and the excitement which prevailed for weeks while the police questioned every suspect.

Not a day passed without its disquieting rumours, and towards the end of the month an incident occurred in Whitechapel which illustrates the terror in which the people lived. It was an incident that might very well have proved of the highest importance to the police, but they seemed doomed to constant disappointment.

At 9.30 in the morning, fully thirty people were standing in George Street when from one of the lodging- houses they heard the cry of murder.

Almost at once a foreign-looking man,

A small crowd ... heard the cry of "Murder," and almost at once a foreign-looking man rushed to the street. In his hand he held a knife. The men were about to close with with when a woman's voice rang out—
"Hold him. It's Jack the Ripper."

of medium size, well dressed, with a dark moustache, came running from the passage into the street. In his hand he held a small knife, but the men about made to close with him, when they heard a woman crying, "Hold him. It's Jack the Ripper."

At these words the men drew back and the foreigner darted past them and along the streets, no one making any attempt to stop him, until he disappeared through some courts a quarter of a mile away.

No sooner had he gone than people in their thousands came running from every direction. The streets were packed with frightened women who had left their homes and their work to seek safety in numbers.

Inside the lodging-house the police found a middle-aged woman, Annie Farmer, who was suffering from a wound in the throat. She had been drinking, and it was not until that afternoon that she was able to make her statement.

Then she told how she had been spoken to by the stranger the previous night, and after a jolly evening, they had gone to the lodging-house but she noticed he scarcely drank at all. In the morning something disturbed her and she moved her head suddenly and felt a knife striking as she thought from behind. She woke and screamed "murder," and the man, who was dressed, ran at once.

Her wound was not serious but the doctors were of the opinion that it had been made by a sudden and strong stroke from behind which had caught her obliquely as she moved her head. It was a miracle she had not been murdered.

The attempt was typical of Jack the Ripper, but the woman, Annie Farmer by name, could give no description of her companion. She could remember practically nothing. Nor could anyone in the lodging-house for the man had kept in the shadows all the time, while those who saw him outside were ashamed to come forward after their display of cowardice.

So what might have been the most valuable clue of all came to nothing. Jack the Ripper was still at large, and day by day the terror grew in every home.

Chapter Five

The crop of letters and postcards purporting to come from Jack the Ripper was heavier than usual following the murder of Marie Kelly in the house in Dorset Street.

Among their number was one which was very similar to the first of its kind, and which, on account of the sequel, attracted considerable attention.

The postcard was received by Mr Saunders the Magistrate at the Thames Police Court, and he at once handed it over to the police for official investigation.

It had been posted in Portsmouth and ran: -

Dear Boss

It is no use for you to look for me in London, because I'm not there. Don't trouble yourself about me until I return, which will not be very long. I like the work too well to leave it alone. Oh, It was such a jolly job the last one. I had plenty of time to do it properly in. Ha, ha, ha! You think it is a man with a black moustache. Ha, ha, ha! When I have done another one, you can try and catch me again.

So, good-bye, dear boss, till I return.

Yours
Jack the Ripper

The handwriting was very like that of the original communications, and the police, as a matter of routine, made inquiries in Portsmouth. News of this leaked out, and caused considerable uneasiness in the seaport town, and the usual precautions against Jack the Ripper were taken.

To allay the public feeling, a message was put out, in which the postcard was described as being in all probability the work of a practical joker, who would be severely dealt with if he could be traced.

No one was prepared for the sequel. That very afternoon an eight year-old lad, Percy Serle, living at Havant, near Portsmouth, was found lying in the street, with four deep wounds in his throat.

He had been playing in the Fair Field

with some companions, and returned along North Street with one of them. The two boys went up a quiet road, and a few minutes later the companion came running down saying that his chum was being murdered.

CRY OF JACK THE RIPPER QUICKLY TAKEN UP

In the busy road the cry of Jack the Ripper was quickly taken up, but when the people reached the spot there was no sign of any assailant while the boy Serle was beyond human aid.

He died a minute or two later without being able to make any statement, but the police acted very promptly in having the roads from Portsmouth and Havant closely watched, while all suspicious persons found at the railway stations about were detained and questioned.

A clasp-knife was found near the body of the lad, while his companion told the police how they had been approached in Mill Lane by a tall, dark man, holding a knife in his hand. Serle had been unable to get away in time, but his friend ran off to fetch the police.

The crime following so rapidly after the anonymous card from Portsmouth, threw the whole town into a state of panic, and there were trepidations of the scenes of terror which had been so common in Whitechapel.

Experts from Scotland Yard came down to make investigations, and though they were satisfied that the murder had nothing to do with Jack the Ripper, yet in their alarm it was very difficult to make the people see this point of view.

The mystery of the unprovoked attack was never solved. The companion of Serle was arrested – a boy of nine – but it was difficult to believe that he could possibly have made the deep wounds with a small knife, and the matter got no further.

The murder was without doubt the act of a person who was simply imitating Jack the Ripper, but it shows clearly the danger to which people were exposed in those dark years. All over the country similar incidents were taking place, and it mattered little whether the real Jack the Ripper was the culprit or not, for the result was the same. Women and children walked in daily fear of being murdered.

A SHOCKING CRIME

Excitement over the Havant affair was at its height when a somewhat similar crime was enacted at Yeobridge, near Yeovil.

This time the victim was a little girl, Emma Davis, just five years of age. At eight o'clock in the morning she had left her parents' little cottage to go and get some milk a mile away. On the way back along the tree-lined road, she was intercepted by the murderer who enticed her into the fields, and dealt with her exactly as Jack the Ripper had dealt with his victims in Whitechapel.

This was enough to spread abroad the fear that he had at last left the East End of London, and was about to embark on a new reign of terror in the provinces, in which helpless little children would be his victims.

It is easy to be wise after the event, and point out how groundless were the fears of mothers who refused to allow their children to go to school even, but at that time, when scarcely a day passed without some outrage or other being reported as possibly the work of Jack the Ripper there was every excuse for their action.

As a matter of fact the Yeobridge murderer was ultimately caught and executed. The night before he was hanged he confessed how the horrors of the Whitechapel crimes had preyed on his mind, and that acting on an overwhelming impulse, he had got up one morning and lurked behind the trees in the lane until the little girl came along.

This quietened public feeling a little, but it was obvious that until Jack the Ripper was laid by the heels, there would be no real feeling of security.

SCOTLAND YARD WORKING DAY AND NIGHT

Behind the scenes Scotland Yard was working day and night sifting out the mass of information which came into their hands, only a small percentage of which was at all reliable. They had, however, reached a point, where they felt reasonably sure of success should Jack the Ripper ever venture again in the East End, and I now propose to disclose what happened at this period.

In their efforts to solve the mystery of the Whitechapel crimes, the police had been given valuable assistance by medical men, and in particular by Dr Forbes Winslow.

The latter had been the first to give as his opinion that the Unknown was a man suffering from homicidal insanity of a temporary nature. In all probability he was quite normal for long periods, but when the madness took possession of him he would go out to kill, and on being restored a day or two later to his proper senses would be quite ignorant of what had transpired in the meantime.

At first the detectives thought this a highly improbable theory and made no effort to test it in any way, but gradually the opinion gained ground that perhaps Dr Winslow was right.

Scotland Yard did not care to admit its changed opinion, and so their next step was kept very private. They got into touch with all the lunatic asylums around London to find if prior to the first murder, any of the inmates suffering from homicidal mania had been liberated as cured. Secondly they wished to know if any such discharged patients had had a medical training.

The inquiries took a long time to make, but at last the detectives discovered that quite a number of patients, who had been under treatment for homicidal insanity, had been at liberty during the months preceding the Whitechapel outrages. None of them, as far as was known, had ever been a doctor or a medical student. The latter point was important, for it was felt that Jack the Ripper possessed more than an elementary knowledge of anatomy.

TWO MEN CLOSELY WATCHED

By tracing the movements of the patients since their discharge, the detectives were able to narrow down the list of possible murderers to two, one of whom was known to live periodically near Shoreditch, while all trace of the other had been lost in the East End.

He was eventually found and the two men were closely watched from that time onwards. The police had absolutely nothing against them and of course, could not question them, although at the same time they made inquiries to see if the suspects could in any way be connected with the murders.

In addition to these two men, information was given to Dr Winslow of the release from a Paris nursing home of a Russian doctor who had made his way to the East End of London just prior to the series of crimes. He had lived the life of a down-and-out, was known to have been in the neighbourhood for over six months, and had often been strange in his manner. He also was marked down as a suspect and detectives were sent to find him.

Lastly, Mr Montague Williams, a former well-known lawyer at the Old Bailey, had been put into possession of a good deal of information which tended to incriminate a notorious character in Whitechapel. I cannot, of course, give the name of this suspect, but there was sufficient evidence regarding his movements at this period to warrant the police taking special measures to keep him under strict survey.

In taking these measures the police had only a faint hope of their ultimate success, relying almost entirely on a different line of enquiry.

Information came to them which turned their attention to the London Docks, but a short walk away from Whitechapel. The exact nature of this information, and its course, I do not profess to know, for never was a secret more jealously guarded by Scotland Yard. It was, however, to the effect that on the night of one of the later crimes, a foreign seaman had been met in the docks and made one or two strange remarks which had a deep significance when, next morning, news of the murder was made known. The information was not passed on until months afterwards, but detectives who made the investigations felt sure they were on the right track.

To find the man concerned was a very difficult task, but the police confined their inquiries to the many cattle boats from foreign ports which put in at the docks. Clearance papers for the previous year were examined, and it was found that no fewer than three of these boats had been lying in dock at different times when the murders had taken place.

The cattlemen on these boats knew enough about anatomy to enable them to carry out the mutilations done by Jack the Ripper. Moreover their boat was the finest hiding place that could have been devised, for no one would suspect them were they seen going about with blood on their clothing.

Narrowing down their inquiries, the police concentrated on one man who had changed his boat on two occasions, but who had certainly been in London at the time of each of the crimes, and who only went ashore at night-time while the boat was lying in dock.

After the Dorset Street murder, he had sailed to a South American port and was expected back at the New Year, 1889. It was essential that nothing should be done that would put him on his guard, and this was the reason for the extraordinary secrecy of Scotland Yard on the matter, who even went to the length of denying that any importance could be placed on the cattle-boat theory.

So matters stood towards the end of 1888, with the whole country, and Whitechapel apprehensive of the next move of Jack the Ripper and with the police quietly confident that his next crime would be his last.

Not for one night had vigilance been relaxed in the dreaded area. The patrols passed round their beats every 15 minutes, the vigilantes worked in co-operation, while the work of lighting up all the dark, forbidding courts and alleys was pushed steadily ahead.

Despite that, a feeling of dread brooded all over the district. The Dorset Street crime had by its atrocity, made a lasting impression and the people wondered what fresh horrors Jack the Ripper had in store for them. Word had been passed round, and found general belief, that he was waiting till Christmas before coming amongst them once again.

The people were "jumpy," ready to take fright at the slightest alarm, wildly exaggerating every little disturbance in the East End. In such a state it is not difficult to imagine the effect produced upon them by the news that another woman had been murdered, this time in Poplar.

At 4.15 on the morning of December 20, a police sergeant on his beat passed along the well-lighted Poplar High Street, and came to a halt outside Clarke's Yard which was used by a carting contractor. Men had been working there until three in the morning, and a constable had looked down it after half-past three, but after hesitating a little, the sergeant decided to make an inspection.

Almost at once he stumbled across the body of a young woman of about 30, lying across the pavement. She was dead. There was no sign of any wound, but acting on instructions from headquarters as to the method to adopt in such a case, the sergeant made no examination but at once summoned doctors and Scotland Yard men.

They hurried to the spot thinking that another Ripper crime had been committed but to their surprise and relief, they discovered that it was of a different nature. The woman had been strangled from behind and the faint marks on her throat indicated that a rope had been drawn round tightly after the manner of a lanyard. No one about had seen the woman entering the yard or heard any sound of a struggle.

The victim was later identified as Rose Mylett, who had been leading a life of shame in Whitechapel, and had fled from there to Poplar in order to be safe from Jack the Ripper.

But though the facts pointed clearly to her having been murdered by some seafaring man, the crime caused an even greater panic in the East End than had the Dorset Street one. The people were in an unreasoning state of terror, the murder was put down to Jack the Ripper, and there were demonstrations and outbursts of feeling all over Poplar.

This would probably have passed away very quickly, but for the action of the authorities at the inquest, who wished only to reassure the public in some way or other.

The doctors, who had been called to the scene, were quite emphatic that Rose Mylett had been strangled, but the police put in as a witness another medical man who had examined the body two days later, and who gave it as his opinion that the woman had died a natural death. This witness was closely associated with Scotland Yard, but his evidence had the opposite effect to that calculated upon.

Instead of calming the public, it made them more uneasy than ever, for they believed that the Yard must have been in possession of some information connecting Jack the Ripper with the crime, otherwise they would never have made such a clumsy attempt to make light of the affair.

In reality the authorities were holding nothing back. They acted in good faith, but prominent detectives with whom I discussed this incident afterwards confessed that it was an ill-considered move and threw a heavy burden on the police, for men had to be drafted into Poplar to quieten the fears of the inhabitants.

DISAPPOINTMENT FOR THE POLICE

Christmas passed with everybody waiting, but nothing was heard of Jack the Ripper. The months went by, with watch still being kept on the suspects, and then came word that the boat the police were waiting for was making for the Port of London.

Directly it put into dock, detectives were instructed to keep the suspect on board under constant surveillance, and if necessary one of the plain clothes men would be signed on as a member of the crew.

To their dismay they discovered that the man they wanted was no longer on the boat. He had left the ship at a port in Spain, and no one knew where he had gone, although it was believed that he had made his way to France and signed on as a cattleman on another boat.

This was the greatest disappointment the police suffered during their quest for Jack the Ripper, and their only hope was that they would be able to get on his track through inquiries by our Consuls on the Continent.

Naturally nothing of this was allowed to leak out, and as the days wore on and still no word of the Terror, the folk in the East End gradually forgot the horrors through which they had passed.

July came, and with it Jack the Ripper.

Once again the crime was committed in Whitechapel in profound silence, and with the same dexterity and force as before. Once again he made his escape in almost miraculous fashion, unseen and unheard, and from his hiding place could laugh at the terror his act had caused.

SPOT WHERE NO STRANGER
DARE VENTURE

Castle Alley, leading off the Whitechapel High Street, was then the lowest quarter of the whole of the East End, and a spot in which no stranger would dare venture after dark. The police had marked Castle Alley as a place to which Jack the Ripper would probably lure one of his victims, and for over nine months a constable had been on duty there with a beat of no more than two hundred yards in extent.

At the beginning of July, in view of the growing confidence, it had been thought safe to extend his beat. So that he passed through the alley every twenty minutes, and immediately that was done Jack the Ripper saw his chance and planned his next crime.

A narrow passage, through which two persons cannot pass abreast, leads from the alley to the main road, striking it at a point just by Aldgate East Railway Station.

At its other end the alley runs into Wentworth Street. Houses backed on to the right side, but a tall hoarding concealed all view of the alley except to those living in the upper rooms. The houses on the left were all in the course of demolition, and practically the only persons with a good view of the place were the superintendent of the public baths and his wife, whose home was at the top end.

The alley was well lighted by a large lamp, which had recently been placed in the centre, but this was not sufficient to deter Jack the Ripper.

At half-past twelve on the morning of July 17, a constable walked through the place. Two vans had been drawn up near the lamp-post, and as it was raining heavily the officer stood in the shelter of one of them and enjoyed a few sandwiches.

He remained there five or six minutes and the echo of his feet had scarcely died away before a police sergeant entered from the Wentworth Street end to see that all was well. He, too, remained a minute or so and saw not a soul. As he was passing into the main road the church clock chimed the three-quarter.

POLICEMAN'S DISCOVERY

Exactly five minutes before, P.C. Andrews came along on his regular beat. Almost at once he saw the woman, lying on the ground beside the lamp-post. Her position in the full light of the lamp, with no attempt at concealment, suggested at once that she was sleeping off the effects of alcohol.

It was not until the officer bent down to shake her to her senses that he saw the awful wounds in her throat, and noticed that her clothing had been disarranged.

In a moment his whistle was blowing and a cordon was quickly thrown round the neighbourhood, the body being left undisturbed until the arrival of Dr Phillips.

He found two characteristic wounds in the throat, severing the arteries and apparently inflicted from behind. One curious fact was that the windpipe had not been cut, and it was possible that the poor woman had cried out for help.

The Terror had only five minutes to lure the woman into Castle Alley and deal with her, and the narrow escape he had from capture was made clear when the body of the victim was examined. An attempt was made at mutilation but almost immediately the murderer had taken alarm and fled, leaving his work uncompleted.

MOST AMAZING FEATURE OF ALL THE CRIMES

How he managed to get away in safety is undoubtedly the most extraordinary feature of all the Ripper crimes.

P.C. Andrews, who made the discovery, had entered the alley from the High Street end. There was only one other way and that was by Wentworth Street, where a watchman was on duty at the gate of his warehouse. He was standing there when the whistles blew and had seen both the first constable and the police sergeant coming out, but no one else.

The wife of the baths superintendent had been standing at her bedroom window at the time, looking down the alley. As luck would have it, she could not see the spot where the body was found, it being obscured from view by the two vans drawn up at the kerb. But she was bound to have seen any man escaping from there.

It seemed that the only possible way of escape was by way of the two little courts leading off the alley, but here again the police were baffled. Both of them were of considerable length but eventually ended in a cul-de-sac. Anyone making down either of them would have been cornered like a rat in a trap, for the police searched them immediately and questioned every person living about without result.

One strange find was made. Beneath the body was found a brightly polished farthing, which in the semi-darkness might well have passed as a sovereign. The detectives recalled the story told to them some time before by a terrified young woman who stated that a foreign looking man had offered her a sovereign to accompany him. Just as she was about to enter the court with him, she had suddenly felt frightened and demanded to see the money.

She snatched it from him, realised how she was being deceived with a polished farthing, and at once ran off, the man making a futile effort to seize her.

DARK FOREIGNER WHO COULD
NOT BE FOUND

No undue importance was placed on this statement at the time, for the police had become used to the hysterical tears of the women in Whitechapel, but now she was interviewed and showed the police officers the polished farthing, and at the same time giving a fuller description of the man.

It was very vague and tallied with the description given of the suspect after the Mitre Square murder. A dark foreigner, speaking English well, with a long moustache, dressed shabbily in black, and of powerful build though only 5ft. 5in. in height.

No one could be found, however, who had seen such a man in the neighbourhood of Castle Alley on the night of the crime.

The speedy identification of the victim brought no help to the harassed detectives.

Alice McKenzie had left her home in Peterborough many years before, and in the East End of London earned an honest living as a charwoman.

The woman had gone to a lodging-house in Gun Street where she knew the deputy, and that night when she made her way out, with her shawl over her head, the deputy had been surprised for she knew that Alice McKenzie did not live on the streets.

Behind the scenes, Scotland Yard had cause to feel annoyed with itself. After eight months of futile shadowing of the list of suspects and careful watch over the docks, it had been decided to discontinue the work in the hope that the last of Jack the Ripper had been heard. Then three weeks after that decision, Alice McKenzie met her death.

There was nothing left but to begin the work all over again. The police were in despair of ever succeeding when word came from Dundee that Jack the Ripper had been caught at last and all their hopes were revived.

The woman, when interviewed, showed the police officers the polished farthing she had been given by the man who tried to lure her away.

Chapter Six

All hopes of catching Jack the Ripper seemed gone when word was flashed from Dundee that roused the people to the highest pitch of expectation. The Terror had committed his last crime in the jute city, and had then gone to the police and confessed everything.

Such reports had often been spread before and been proved to have no foundation, but in this instance the facts were so curious as to demand the closest investigation. Detectives were sent up from Scotland Yard but no statement was ever made regarding the outcome of their inquiries, and when William Henry Bury paid the penalty for his crime on the scaffold, opinion was divided as to whether he was really Jack the Ripper, or was only suffering from delusions.

The few officials who were in possession of the full facts maintained such an extraordinary secrecy that it was a long time before I was able to discover what had gone on behind the scenes in Dundee, and the reason why public curiosity was never satisfied.

The whole story is very interesting for there were certainly strong grounds for believing that William Henry Bury was the Whitechapel murderer.

At the beginning of January, a rather small but powerfully built man boarded the steamer Cambria lying at the London docks, and was accompanied by a middle-aged woman whom he said was his wife. Mr and Mrs Bury were apparently on good terms with one another, but it was noticed by the other passengers that neither of them would speak about their past life, except that they had left their home in the East End of London and intended setting up home in Dundee.

From the first the man was very anxious about his luggage, particularly about a large and heavy wooden case which he was taking with him, and which had just been whitewashed.

They seemed to have plenty of money, and on their arrival in Dundee they were at a loss where to go, having no friends in the city and never having been there before.

Bury went in search of lodgings and it was some time before he found a satisfactory place, finally renting two rooms in the basement of a tenement house at 113 Princes Street. Neighbours saw very little of them, although they spent a good deal of money on drink.

SHUT HIMSELF UP IN THE BASEMENT

A little over a fortnight had passed when Mrs Bury apparently disappeared while her husband shut himself up in the basement where he could be heard occasionally walking about. He came out on two or three occasions and was then noticed to be under the influence of drink.

At the end of that week he made his way from the house and with bloodshot eyes and uncertain footsteps, entered the Central Police Office and approached Lieutenant Parr.

"What do you want?" he was asked.

"I'm Jack the Ripper and I want to give myself up," was the startling reply.

The lieutenant believed at first he was dealing with a madman but he signed to another officer to stand by in readiness, then asked the man why he called himself Jack the Ripper.

"I'm him all right," Bury replied, "and if you go along to my house in Princes Street you'll find the body of a woman packed up in a box and cut up."

He was detained at once, but would give no information beyond the number of the house where at which the body was found and his own name and occupation, describing himself as a sawdust merchant.

When the officers forced an entry into the basement they found the first room quite bare. Passing into the next room there was only a small bed on which a heap of clothes had been piled, while in the corner stood a large white-washed packing case. In this was wedged the dismembered trunk of a woman.

At once the affair assumed the greatest

importance, provided that the murder was not merely an imitative one.

DUNDEE POLICE IN TOUCH WITH SCOTLAND YARD

Bury was charged and questioned, and adhered to his confession. In addition he gave the address in Whitechapel at which he had last been staying before taking the boat to Dundee, and said that it would be found he was in the East End at the time of all the crimes, and the police could find evidence against him if they wished.

The Dundee police at once got into touch with Scotland Yard and a dozen experienced men were sent to make the necessary inquiries.

At first they were very successful. Bury's last landlord was traced and he had an unusual story to tell.

As far as he knew the woman was Bury's wife and was the daughter of a London tradesman, but he did not know where her parents resided. Bury had always described himself as a sawdust merchant and latterly had grown very strange in his manner.

He had been consistently cruel to his wife, but she was uncomplaining, and never used to dare ask him where he had been when he absented himself at night.

In the end Bury had expressed the greatest anxiety to get away from London and booked his passage to Dundee. He did not tell his landlord this, but made out that he and his wife had decided to emigrate to Brisbane.

A few days before his leave-taking he had told his landlord to make him a strong case, and he produced the measurements of the box he wanted. He was very particular about this, but would not say what it was for, beyond that it would be for packing some of his possessions, although the landlord was well aware that the couple had nothing to take away except their clothing.

ALWAYS PLENTY OF MONEY

Bury paid for the case and had always plenty of money to spare, while he carried about with him a large amount of jewellery on which subject the landlord was careful to ask no questions.

Most of the jewellery had been sold in Dundee, but even at the time of his arrest Bury still wore on his fingers several valuable rings which would have provided him with funds to have made an attempt to escape from the country had he desired.

The explanation of the crime as far as he would ever tell it was not altogether in keeping with his assertion that he was Jack the Ripper.

According to his story, he and his wife were on the best of terms, but on the Monday night before his arrest they had been out having a good time, and he could not even remember going to bed.

In the morning he woke up, and to his horror found his wife lying dead beside him. She had been strangled with a cord.

He could recollect nothing of what had happened and did not know whether he had committed the crime or whether it had been done by someone else, but realising the danger of the position he had set to work to dispose of the body. With a sharp and finely ground knife which he happened to have in his possession he had dismembered the body and placed it in the case, ready for removal.

His mind was in such a ferment that he went out and got drunk and the days which followed were a constant nightmare, with the body of his wife ever beside him and with him unable to think of a way out of his position. He had kept drinking to try and forget until his nerves at last failed him and he had gone to the police.

WOULD MAKE NO DISCLOSURES

This account, which he gave after he had been in prison for some time, was all that he would ever disclose to the police and it gave the impression that he had reflected on his dangerous position and wished to appear in the most favourable light possible.

Directly the London police had traced his landlord, he was asked why he had had the box made, and why he had told the maker he was going to Australia. He made no reply, nor would he explain how the jewellery had come into his possession and why he had gone to Dundee when there was no possibility of business as a sawdust merchant.

Information about his wife or himself he simply would not give, but naturally the most interest centred round the question as to whether he was Jack the Ripper.

Working backwards, the police, I afterwards learned, had established the fact that he was missing from his lodgings on the night that Marie Kelly was done to death in her home in Dorset Street, and that he had been in the habit of carrying that knife about with him. His description was very like that of the man who had been speaking to the young woman Kelly on the night of the crime, and the Scotland Yard men who travelled north tried to get a statement from him.

Nothing could make Bury speak. He admitted that he had described himself as Jack the Ripper, but his attitude was that the police would have to get their own information.

No one knew where he had stayed in the East End prior to going to his new land-lord's home, and if he carried on a business as a sawdust merchant the police were certainly never able to verify it.

They did find, in the end, that Bury had originally come from Wolverhampton, where he had made a precarious living by selling lead pencils and toy rings in the street. He left the town and was not seen again until just after the time of the first Whitechapel murder, when he brought with him the woman he called his wife.

He was very prosperous, with plenty of jewellery, and cashed on one occasion a note for £50. It was then he first described himself as a sawdust merchant, and said his wife was the daughter of an East London publican, but beyond that he gave his relatives no information whatever.

Going back to London he had apparently constantly changed his address and although the police were able to trace several of these, there were important gaps in his history which they could never fill.

They kept their own counsel, and when Bury came up for trial it was the common opinion that he was guilty of the Whitechapel crimes and would make a full confession in the event of his being condemned to death.

It was even expected that he would make a statement at his trial, but the mystery was not to be solved in such easy fashion. He took the sentence calmly, and even discussed the possibilities of a reprieve.

In such a mood he was not likely to help the police, and, thwarted at every turn the Scotland Yard men began to incline to the opinion that his confession was a bogus one. On the other hand, certain aspects of the Princes Street crime were very similar to those committed in Whitechapel. In height and build he answered the description of the suspect seen after two of the murders. The knife that the Terror used was probably just such a one as that carried about by Bury, and on one occasion when he was definitely known to be staying in the East End at the time of a Ripper crime, he had absented himself from the house for that night in the most suspicious manner. Finally, and this carried a great deal of weight with ordinary people, he was in the habit of walking about very quietly and had often frightened people by his silent approach.

Against that was the fact that he did not look much like a foreigner, such as witnesses had described, and it was possible that the crime had a totally different explanation from what most people believed.

MIGHT HAVE BEEN ENGAGED IN AN UNLAWFUL CALLING

Bury was not a sawdust merchant, and the secretiveness with which he and his wife went about their activities in London, suggested that it might have some connection with the large amount of jewellery he was constantly handling. It was, therefore, possible that he had been engaged in an unlawful calling, and Mrs Bury had threatened to expose him. Out of fear he had devised the plan to rid himself of her in Dundee.

It was a plausible theory, and the police

had kept it in view from the beginning.

But yet another discovery was made. The home of Bury in the East End at the time of the Hanbury Street murder was traced, and again it was ascertained that on that night Bury had kept away from his home, and his manner on his return home the next afternoon suggested a madman.

Nothing of this was made public, but in official circles it was hoped that Bury himself would confess the whole truth before his death.

On the day before his execution two detectives were sent from London to be present should he make a last statement. This I myself only learned years afterwards, so carefully guarded was the secret, but it shows the importance Scotland Yard attached to their discoveries.

Bury disappointed them. He did ask to see a clergyman to whom he made a communication which was passed on to the Marquis of Lothian, then Secretary for Scotland, but it was never made public.

EXPRESSED REGRET FOR MURDER
OF HIS WIFE

I know he expressed regret for the murder of his wife, gave further details of what happened in the house in Princes Street, and while volunteering a few more particulars concerning himself, he declined to say any more about Mrs Bury, whose identity remained a mystery.

Scotland Yard concentrated on the personal details given to them. At first the facts they gathered pointed more and more clearly to Bury being Jack the Ripper, but it was a slow task, entailing months of work, and they had been ordered to make nothing public.

They established where he had been staying on the nights of three other of the Whitechapel murders, and from the recollection of those who lived nearby, it was quite possible that he had the opportunity to commit them. In addition he had periodical outbursts of almost maniacal anger in which he cruelly ill-treated his wife and often threatened to use the knife on her. At such times he was very strange in his behaviour

and people were afraid to approach him.

All the evidence was entirely circumstantial, with opinion at the Yard sharply divided as to whether Bury was the guilty man or not. Such information as was available never reached the public, who believed that Bury had made a full confession of the crimes.

Those in authority were quite content that this should be so, for it is a notable fact that at this period there were no more outrages and alarms throughout the kingdom, as though the execution of the Dundee murderer had removed the long period of terror in which the people had lived.

There was another reason for the official silence, which a well-known detective of that time confided in me. In spite of the organisation at their command, Scotland Yard had really failed to trace the complete history of Bury, and although they were quite blameless in the affair yet there would be a further loss of confidence if that became generally known.

NO FURTHER REPORT OF
JACK THE RIPPER

As it was, they could congratulate themselves, as month after month passed by and there was no further report of Jack the Ripper.

Watch was still being kept on the cattle boats and on those suspects whom I discussed in the last chapter, but nothing of importance was learned.

The summer went by with the alarms in the East End becoming more and more rare, until a disquieting discovery was made in a street, which was in the very heart of the Ripper crimes.

While passing along Backchurch Lane at half-past five in the morning, a constable stumbled across a parcel lying in the shadow of the railway arches, and which had certainly not been there when he passed by 20 minutes before.

It contained the dismembered body of a woman of about 30 years of age, and had evidently been mutilated by a left-handed person who possessed a good knowledge of anatomy.

Dr Phillips, who was once more summoned, gave it as his opinion that the wounds were practically identical with those inflicted on Marie Kelly, except that there was no evidence of wantonness. The woman had been dead for four days and had undoubtedly been the victim of violence.

The police measures had been so perfected that within three hours of the discovery every cattle boat in the docks had been visited and the crews interrogated, but each individual was able to give a satisfactory account of his movements the previous night.

It is an interesting sidelight on the Ripper crimes as showing that the police still believed that the Terror would one day be traced to one of these boats.

DREAD AND UNCERTAINTY AGAIN

As can be expected, this fresh outrage threw the whole neighbourhood into a state of dread and uncertainty, which was not very much lessened when at the inquest on the woman whose identity remained unknown, the Coroner, Mr Baxter, after reviewing the whole of the detailed medical evidence said, "It is a matter of congratulation that this crime does not seem to have any connection with the previous murders in the neighbourhood."

This was the fifth murder of this type which had occurred in London in the space of a few months and it was no consolation to the people to be told that it was not the work of Jack the Ripper, when there was another and even more deadly criminal at work amongst them.

The whole of that winter was spent in expectation of further atrocities which happily did not eventuate, and it was not until February 13, 1891, that the Ripper was heard of again.

His escape on this occasion must have been the narrowest he had ever known, but once more he disappeared into space without the slightest sound to mark his flight.

The discovery was made in circumstances with which the people had grown only too familiar.

More troublesome for the police than any other spot in the neighbourhood of Leman Street Police Station was the narrow road known as Swallow Gardens.

Along one side ran the railway arches for a length of almost fifty yards. Boarded up, they were used as warehouses, and facing them was a line of dilapidated houses, mostly tenanted by women of questionable reputation.

It was lit only at its ends, the middle part being in complete darkness. A number of attempts had been made to place a lamp in the centre of Swallow Gardens, but it was invariably damaged beyond repair almost at once.

Railway employees used it at night to get to their work, while it was frequently used by local people who wished to take the short cut down to the docks. In spite of this, it had a very bad reputation and the police patrolled it regularly.

WHAT A RAILWAYMAN SAW

Soon after midnight the police had to take a couple of young women into custody as a result of trouble with seafaring men. They cleared the street of curious sightseers and kept a close watch on it until the trouble had died down.

At about 1.45 a.m. a young railwayman was passing along the Gardens when he noticed a young woman, none too well dressed, approaching in the company of a foreign looking man, who was dressed in a long, light coat, and who kept his head averted.

The railwayman noticed that they were loitering about as though they were not certain where to go, and a few minutes later they were seen again in the neighbourhood.

Apparently one of them at least had no wish to be seen by a policeman, for when the patrolling constable made his way down the Gardens just a few minutes before two, there was no sign of the couple.

Everything was quite clear, and it was not until ten minutes past two that he again entered the road.

All was quiet, but he could not see clearly past the light of the lamp at the beginning of the road. It was not until he

A railwayman noticed a young woman in the company of a foreign-looking man who kept his head averted.

had left it behind him that he at once distinguished a motionless form in the centre of the roadway, opposite the railway arches.

He ran to the spot, and found a young woman of 25 gasping her life away, but though he kept his eye on the further end of Swallow Gardens he could see no one making his escape.

TREMENDOUS FORCE USED

The young woman had been wounded in the throat, her assailant having used tremendous force and severed the jugular vein. Even as the constable knelt down beside her he noticed that she was still alive.

She seemed to open her eyes, and he stooped down to catch any words she might utter, but almost at once she passed away. From the nature of the wound it could only have been inflicted in a matter of seconds before, yet the Terror had gotten clean away.

The whistle of the constable brought immediate assistance, and soon Dr Phillips was examining once more the dire work of the man the police could not catch.

Evidently the Ripper had been disturbed immediately by the arrival of the constable and before he could commence the usual mutilation.

The victim was lying with her feet crossed and against the footpath. Her black crepe hat was beside her and her clothing disarranged slightly.

While the examination proceeded every house in the street was searched, for it seemed impossible that the murderer had made good his escape in any other way than that of taking refuge in one of those buildings. A cordon of police kept the rapidly increasing crowd at a distance, rushing wildly there as the dread name passed from lip to lip.

A cordon was drawn round the docks and no cattle boat allowed to leave until every member of the crew had established his innocence.

One curious discovery was made by the detectives. Pinned to the frock of the victim and hidden by her shawl, they found an old black hat. She had evidently been wearing the new one lying in the roadway and assuming that she had bought it only a short time previously, and would not throw away the old one, it would be a simple matter to trace the shop where the sale had been made, and from that discovery the identity of the victim.

The inquiry was at once successful. Not only did the police obtain the information they wanted, but the clue led them to a man who at last seemed to be the one who had eluded them so long.

Chapter Seven

The scenes in Whitechapel following the discovery in Swallow Gardens were truly remarkable. The narrow street was crowded with people, and the police were kept busy rescuing women and children who were in danger of being badly injured in the crush.

There was good reason for the excitement. The rumour had passed round that Jack the Ripper had taken refuge in one of the tenements in the street, and the police were certain to catch him that morning.

As I related previously, it seemed impossible that the Terror could have made his escape without being seen by the constable, and the only conclusion was that he had run into one of the tenements, each of which had been kept closely guarded. A quick search had been made during the night, but there was still the possibility that he was lurking in some dark spot, waiting his chance to make a dash for freedom.

In the morning a more thorough search was started with the huge crowd waiting breathlessly for the arrest. The possibility of taking him from the police and dealing with him on the spot was being discussed. Suddenly a little man came running out of a doorway towards them. He had been disturbed by the detectives while sleeping in a shed at the back of the houses and had instinctively run off at their approach.

No sooner did the crowd catch sight of him that with one cry of "Jack the Ripper" they turned to get away from him, and a number of women were knocked down and injured in the stampede for safety.

The suspect was caught almost at once by the police, and proved to have no connection with the murder, but the incident shows to what an extent the inhabitants of the East End had been terrorised by Jack the Ripper that the very sight of him would make thousands turn tail and run.

Nothing was gained by the search but the detectives who were inquiring among shopkeepers for the young woman who had purchased the new black hat, found by the body of the victim, met with immediate success.

AN IMPORTANT CLUE

In a little shop in Spitalfields they came upon the woman who had sold the hat.

On the previous afternoon, a young woman, whom she knew as Frances Coles had bought the hat for five shillings. Earlier in the week she had tried to get it on payment of a small sum in advance, but on her second call she said she had found a friend who was willing to lend her the money.

The shop-keeper noticed a man loitering nearby, but as he kept his head turned away she could not describe him beyond saying that he was middle-aged, of thick-set build and fairly well-dressed.

Frances Coles, whom she knew lived in Thrawl Street, Spitalfields, (where other of Jack the Ripper's victims had lodged), was anxious to wear the hat at once. She put it on and carefully pinned the old one to her dress, remarking that it would come in handy in some way or other.

When she left she was joined further down the road by the middle-aged man.

It was a simple matter to confirm the identification of Frances Coles.

The deputy at the lodging-house described her as a very quiet, nice-looking young woman, of a superior type who had only recently taken to life in the East End. He was able to relate a curious incident that had taken place the night before.

After being out all day, Frances Coles returned about eleven at night, going straight through to the kitchen without a word to anyone. There she sat with her head in her arms, and about half an hour later a man called to see her.

His description tallied with that of the man outside the shop, but when he asked to see the girl Coles, he was covering his face with his hand, and it was bleeding rather badly.

HAD BEEN ATTACKED BY ROUGHS

He explained that he had been attacked by some roughs who had knocked him down and stolen all his money and his watch.

"If I find the woman who told them to do it, I'll do her in for sure," he said, going into the kitchen.

There he remained talking to the girl Coles for over an hour and was heard to leave about twenty to one, but no one saw him go.

The girl went out half an hour afterwards and at twenty to two was seen alone at a little grocery store, where she came in for some bread, but owing to some words with the shopkeeper she was turned away. At that time she would be within a quarter of a mile of Swallow Gardens where she was found murdered half an hour later.

At three o'clock the deputy was surprised to see the man back again. He was in a state of excitement and covered with blood.

"I've been knocked down and robbed in the Ratcliffe Highway," he told the deputy, and seemed taken aback when the latter replied, "How could they rob you when you had lost all your money before?" "Oh," he said, "they thought they were going to get something, but they were mistaken."

He was very anxious to get a bed, but owing to his appearance he was refused admission and advised to go to the London Hospital to have his injuries attended to. As far as the deputy could make out he had been struck on the head, but though there was much blood on him the deputy could see no real wound.

The police found that a man had called the hospital and complained of damaged ribs. The doctor found nothing really wrong with him except a small cut over the eye which must have bled very freely indeed to account for the state of his clothing. As he was somewhat dazed he was allowed to lie down on a couch for an hour until he was well enough to take his leave. He gave the impression of being a sea-faring man, and inquiries were made at the docks by the now excited detectives.

THE TRAIL PICKED UP AGAIN

Once more his trail was picked up. At two o'clock in the morning, two constables had come across him, and on being asked where he was making for, he said some dock labourers had attacked him and he believed some of his ribs were broken. They made a rough examination, found him quite sound, and as a third officer came along, he was allowed to go and was last seen making in the direction of Swallow Gardens, eight or nine minutes walk away.

Furthermore, it was learned that immediately after the time of the murder, he had made another attempt to get into the docks but had been seen and turned away.

At last it looked as if the police theory were to be proved correct. Jack the Ripper was employed on one of the boats, and, unable to get to his refuge as he had planned, he had been forced to go to the lodging-house in Thrawl Street only to be again disappointed.

The police, at this stage of their inquiries, were convinced that he had deliberately planned the death of Frances Coles after his first meeting with her earlier in the day. Before he could carry out his design he had been the victim of some hooligans, but with his purpose still fixed in his mind, he had left behind him the clues that were to lead to his capture.

All London was agog with the news that the Ripper could no longer evade arrest and that Sunday the detectives were hampered on every hand by the curious crowds who watched their every movement. The change in public opinion was shown when the superintendent in charge of the case was cheered whenever he made his appearance.

JACK THE RIPPER REPORTED IN CUSTODY

Late that night, the news, for which everyone was waiting, was passed round. Jack the Ripper was in custody in Leman Street Police Station.

The arrest had been effected without any fuss. Two detectives called at a public house in Whitechapel, and walking up to a short, thick-set man who was drinking by himself, tapped him on the shoulder.

"Are you James Thomas Sadler?" he was asked.

He was startled, but admitted that he was. At a signal from one of the detectives, other plain clothes men entered the bar and Sadler was escorted to the police station and there charged with the murder of Frances Coles.

His identity and whereabouts had been established in a strange fashion.

During the evening the police had been visited by a sailor named Duncan Campbell, who told how on that morning he had met a stranger in the Sailors' Home who had sold him a big clasp knife for sixpence. It was such a bargain that Campbell bought it on the spot, but when he opened it later he thought there were bloodstains on it.

At once he connected it with Jack the Ripper, but thought he was being fanciful. At the same time he could not bear to handle the knife any longer and sold it to a dealer for two shillings. He could not give the name of the man who had sold him the knife, but in the past he had occasionally stayed at the Sailors' Home.

One official recalled the suspect and gave his name as Sadler. In the docks a boat was found in which a James Thomas Sadler had been one of the crew, but he had been paid off and no one knew where he was.

Luck was with the police. Almost as soon as he left the station, Campbell ran into the suspect and watched him enter the public house where he was arrested.

STOUTLY PROTESTED HIS INNOCENCE

From the first Sadler stoutly protested his innocence. He gave particulars concerning himself, and said that on the night of the murder he had not seen Frances Coles again from the time he left her at twenty to one in the lodging-house.

When he appeared in court to answer the charge that was expected to be but the forerunner of many others, a huge crowd gathered outside to demonstrate against him. There were cries of "Jack the Ripper," and mothers held up their children to get a glimpse of the dreaded man. Kept back by the strong guard of police the crowd gave vent to a storm of hissing and booing and Sadler seemed to lose his nerve.

No one doubted but that he was the right man.

A witness had been found who gave details of his history, which made the case against him very black indeed. A married man with five children, his wife was living apart from him in Kent, and it was alleged that this was on account of his brutal behaviour.

A seafaring man, he knew every inch of Whitechapel, and up to 1888 had made his home in Buck's Row, the scene of the earliest Ripper crime. On that night, it was stated, he had suddenly disappeared only to reappear at each of the following murders.

This statement was made public – a thing impossible under present conditions, and feeling against Sadler was very high. Sketches of him in court appeared in every paper, and a full description of him given with the result that any number of people came forward to say they had seen such a man loitering at the scene of each of the Whitechapel murders.

As far as the police inquiries went into his past history, they certainly discovered he had been living by Buck's Row and had gone from there suddenly, and he was also back in London at the time of three of the murders, but whether he was at sea when the others were committed could not be learned for some time.

A POSITION OF GREAT GRAVITY

The hostility shown to Sadler at the police court frightened him and he realised the gravity of his position. From prison he managed to get a letter smuggled out, a letter in which he made a pathetic appeal for fair play.

A few citizens who felt that there was too much prejudice against him made inquiries, and it was established beyond all doubt that the statement made giving details of his "reappearance" in London was very inaccurate and had been made in malice. Furthermore, there was a ring of truth about his story of his movements on the night of the murder, and his helpers saw that he was now legally represented.

In his statement he related how he had met the girl, how she had bought the hat with his money, and had parted in the evening on the understanding that he would meet her again in the lodging-house.

He was coming to keep that appointment when he was attacked and robbed. After seeing her, he wanted to get back to his boat to sleep there for the night, but at the docks he was refused admission and was struck by a dock labourer whom he called a dock rat.

It was just after this that he was spoken to by the police, and then, when he was wandering about, he was attacked once more and badly knocked about. When he recovered he came back to the lodging-house only to be told to go to the hospital. While on his way there he ran into the cordon of police and was actually searched for any knife he might have. He had none and was allowed to go on.

This story was corroborated in every detail. He denied having sold a clasp knife to Duncan Campbell, and the latter, under pressure, admitted that it might have been another man altogether and in any case he merely imagined the blood-stains. Campbell confessed that like most people at that time, his thoughts were so full of terror at the crimes of Jack the Ripper, that he was ready to jump to any conclusion when he was shown a knife.

A QUESTION OF TIME

When the police had completed their case against Sadler it was found that it hinged on the time when the sailor had been seen by the constables at the docks.

Two of the officers were certain that Sadler had left them just as the church clock was striking two, and had made his way in the direction of Swallow Gardens. It was contended that he had encountered Frances Coles there, and blaming her for his being robbed, had cut her throat.

The third constable, however, was just as sure that the clock was striking the quarter, by which time the murder had been committed.

In addition all the evidence went to prove that Sadler had been in a dazed and semi-helpless condition that night and could not possibly have murdered the girl and got away quickly and in silence.

In the face of this there was nothing to do but liberate Sadler. This was deferred a few days until public feeling had died down somewhat, a precaution that had also been found necessary in the case of "Leather Apron."

Once again the police came in for severe criticism in allowing Jack the Ripper to slip through their fingers so easily, but the real mistake that had been made was never made known.

I have referred before to their strong belief that he would eventually be found to be employed on one of the cattle boats that put in at the docks. Following the plan they had worked out, the docks were closely watched directly news of the Swallow Gardens crime reached them.

EVERY BOAT SECRETLY SEARCHED

Every boat was being thoroughly, but secretly searched when they learned about Sadler, and, thinking they were after the right man, the general search was abandoned, and all efforts concentrated on hunting down the suspect. Almost a dozen boats were allowed to leave the Thames without the crews having been questioned, before the police realised they had got the wrong man again.

In the East End the people were as scared as ever they had been. An instance of this was provided at the funeral of Frances Coles when the streets were filled with curious sightseers. At one point in East Ham a stampede occurred when a man ran along shouting that Jack the Ripper had committed another murder close by, but the police, however, soon had the situation in hand.

The deputy of the lodging-house in Thrawl Street, who had seen Sadler and the girl, was taken seriously ill when he read that Sadler was really Jack the Ripper. For two years he had been living in dread that the Terror would one night come to his lodging-house, and the thought that he had been alone with the Ripper for some time brought on a shock from which he died.

With people living in such a state of nervous tension, it is not surprising that there was a recurrence of the scenes which were now familiar to the police.

The vigilantes, numbering many hundreds, resumed their patrols, but they made no attempt to co-operate with the police, and it was as if the majority of them were thinking only of the rewards which had again been offered by private persons.

Each constable was on the alert. The Thames division was composed of the best men in the Metropolitan Police, for it was an open secret that the man who captured Jack the Ripper would be "made" for life, and it was the ambition of every enterprising officer to get transferred to the division where the Ripper was operating.

NUMBERS OF FALSE ALARMS

There were plenty of false alarms, but interest was quickly centred in the West End when four young women in quick succession were waylaid in the streets and stabbed slightly.

This was followed by a murder almost typical of Jack the Ripper, when Augustine Dawes, aged 26, was found lying in Holland Park Road soon after midnight with her throat cut.

An artist actually saw the murderer bending over the girl after the crime, evidently bent to copy the East End Terror. He shouted for help but the guilty man made his escape unmolested.

Some days later he was arrested at Belturbet, in Ireland, and the disclosure of the whole facts caused the greatest uneasiness.

Related to titled Irish families, the young man had been for years mentally unstable, and because of his violent conduct had to be sent to an institution near London. From this he escaped, taking with him a knife and the attendants knew that for some time he had been talking a great deal about doing what Jack the Ripper had done.

He got away without the matter being reported to the police and it was only after reading about the Kensington murder that his relatives grew anxious. He was traced to Ireland and by his conduct on the way there could be no doubt he was the guilty man.

The disquieting feature of the case was that it was established that since 1888 he had several times made his escape from the institution and had been roaming about London for days before being captured and each time the matter was kept quiet.

He was found to be unfit to take his trial and was kept in detention, but there was a demand made for a stricter supervision of private institutions.

It will be remembered that some long time before, Dr Winslow had suggested that the crimes were the work of a man suffering from homicidal mania who was not being kept in proper restraint. The police, after much prompting, had got into touch with every mental institution around London to try and trace such a man without success.

Here then, was an instance of a young man, capable of committing the crimes, who had been at liberty on several occasions (but not, I must make clear, at the time of any of the Whitechapel murders), and the matter had never been reported.

It was possible that there were other cases and, in fact, it was learned that escapes from private homes were quite common, which if they had been reported might have led the police to the right man.

For several months after the Kensington affair alarming rumours were spread about homicidal lunatics being at large, and every town in the country was subjected to scares.

It has often been stated that the police knew for certain that Jack the Ripper was a German. In view of the recent outrages in Dusseldorf, the origin of this statement is interesting.

After the Swallow Gardens murder the German town of Frankfurt was thrown into panic by the murder of five women the type of victim and the mutilations being precisely similar to those in the East End.

The guilty man was never discovered, but at the request of the English authorities a full report of the crimes was sent to Scotland Yard and from the smaller details which had been known only to the police, the Coroner and the doctors who made the examination, there was every ground for believing it might be the same man.

Only by a personal examination could this be made certain but on the ground of expense, nothing further was done. When some years later, there was no further fear of Jack the Ripper returning, detectives remembering this report in which it stated that the murderer was known to speak German fluently and it seemed quite possible that Jack the Ripper had fled to Germany when London grew too hot for him. Their opinion that it might be the same man has been passed on until there are now many people who regard it as a disputable fact.

But whatever the police might think, the people still clung to the curious belief that the Terror would commit twelve murders and then give himself up, and until that time came they demanded every possible protection. The patrols were as numerous as ever, and on every hand the people were discussing where and when the next blow would fall.

Chapter Eight

The years of terror were drawing to an end. Since the murder of Frances Coles and the narrow escape of James Sadler, nothing further had been heard of Jack the Ripper, and he had vanished completely. The large rewards still offered for information about him remained unclaimed, and the unending police inquiries brought no success.

But though month succeeded month and still no sign from him, the dread in which the people had lived was slow in dying.

Holiday times in particular brought reminders of his work, and at the end of a day's outing on Hampstead Heath or at Epping Forest, families banded together to make their way home in safety through the East End.

Nobody who lived at that time will forget the great scare in the spring of 1893, when the rumour passed throughout London that Jack the Ripper had returned and murdered a little girl in East Ham.

In a matter of a few hours every school child and every mother in the city had heard the story, and they had no doubt it was true.

The mothers in their thousands rushed to the schools to escort the children home and the little ones trembled in fear, despite the efforts of the school teachers to reassure everybody. Suspicion that day fell on any man who spoke to a school child, and several cases of mobbing by angry parents were reported.

Although the rumour was promptly denied the scare lasted for a long time, for the children had been thoroughly terrified by the mad stampede that afternoon, and many of them could not be persuaded to return to school. These alarms among the youngsters occurred periodically until just before the war and was perhaps the effect of the Whitechapel crimes. Twenty-five years after he had last made himself known in the East End, the name of Jack the Ripper could still arouse the old-time fears.

In other respects the people were gradually getting back to a normal state of mind. The flow of threatening letters signed "Jack the Ripper," had almost ceased, and the number of imitative crimes had diminished greatly.

They were still occurring in various parts of the country, and one instance in London shows how all classes of people were affected.

YOUNG WOMAN'S STARTLING EXPERIENCE

A young woman living in the Waterloo Road was accosted after midnight by a very well-dressed man, who some time later drew out a knife, and saying, "I'm Jack the Ripper," attempted to murder her.

Fortunately the girl escaped with only a slight wound, and the man was afterwards arrested. It was then discovered that he was the son of one of the most prominent citizens of London, who had been, until that night perfectly normal in his manner.

When sentenced to a short term of imprisonment he told how he had been fascinated by the accounts of the White-chapel atrocities, and night after night he could not sleep for thinking about them. At last one night he could not bear it any longer and crept out of his home in the West End. After getting a knife from the kitchen, he wandered about until he met the girl.

His story was a perfectly genuine one, and in his case, Jack the Ripper brought about the ruin of his career.

Even more terrifying was the experience of a Croydon family who were in danger of being murdered in their sleep by the father of the house, who was discovered walking into his daughter's bedroom with a knife in his hand and muttering, "Jack the Ripper has come at last."

The man was walking in his sleep and was quite unaware of what he was doing and when told could scarcely believe it was true. He confessed, however, that for years he had been suffering from nightmares as a result of what he had read in the newspapers.

ENDED WHERE IT BEGAN

It is a strange thing that the reign of terror may be said to have come to a definite end with the murder of Marie Damyon in

Thomas Street, Whitechapel, a turning off Buck's Row, where Jack the Ripper claimed his first victim.

The widow of a blacksmith, she had gone to stay with a Miss Matthews, recently married, who lived in two rooms over a coffee shop.

In the early hours of the morning Miss Matthews was awakened by a scream of terror, and then came a cry of, "Sarah, Sarah!"

She recognised the voice of the woman Damyon, and was about to run out to her bedroom, and see what had happened when she heard a knocking at the door of her room.

In opening it Marie Damyon fell into her arms, suffering from two severe wounds to her throat.

She died almost immediately, and the affair caused the utmost consternation in the neighbourhood, for, being unaware of all the facts, the people thought that the Ripper had returned at last.

Huge crowds gathered outside the house and the scanty reports that appeared in the Sunday papers certainly pointed to yet another series of murders, and the scenes in Whitechapel that followed were reminiscent of those which followed the double crime in Berner Street and Mitre Square.

To the police the affair was no mystery. They learned that Miss Matthews' husband had been about the street on the previous night and was missing. Furthermore he had only recently been discharged from a lunatic asylum and that evening he was arrested at his sister's home in Hackney.

His behaviour marked him as insane and he boasted that he had "killed Marie." although he had no dislike for her at all. Unable to plead before a court, he was declared insane and detained during Her Majesty's pleasure.

As soon as it became evident that Marie Damyon was not the victim of the Ripper, the relief was tremendous, and there were even thanksgiving services of a hysterical kind held in streets in the East End.

On every hand people declared that Jack the Ripper had gone for good, and as events turned out their instinct was right.

There was good ground for their belief. It was founded on the fact that since the first murder by Jack the Ripper there had been no serious crimes in the East End except those committed by him.

Even prior to the appearance of Jack the Ripper, the East End of London was notorious for the brutal crimes that took place there, and so it is really remarkable that for almost six years there were none other than those I have recorded in this series.

There is little doubt that this peaceful attitude on the part of the criminals infesting the area was entirely due to fear of the consequences.

HOPELESS TO EXPECT MERCY

Quite apart from the danger due to the presence of the extra police in the district, any would-be murderer would naturally shrink from committing a crime which would throw suspicion on him being the Terror. Even if he escaped that peril it would be useless for him to expect any mercy, with public feeling aroused to such a dangerous pitch.

This has been widely commented upon by responsible people, and the Thomas Street murder was seized upon as proof that the East End was once more normal and that Jack the Ripper had gone.

To me it is a curious example of crowd psychology, but in concluding that the Terror had gone, the people were right.

Nothing more was ever heard of him. At intervals wild rumours swept through the country, but no longer were they accepted without question; nor no longer did they cause panic.

From the day that Marie Damyon met her death, not another case was reported to Scotland Yard of men trying to imitate Jack the Ripper.

Women and children felt safe at last, but the memory of those long years had left its mark, and the name of the Terror was recalled only in dread.

Until 1897 the police combined their special inquiries and observations at the docks, still hoping that the Terror would walk into the traps they had laid.

They learned nothing new. British representatives abroad were instructed to report on any rumours of Jack the Ripper they might hear, but he had vanished completely.

Since then it has been hoped that a death-bed confession might clear up the mystery, but if he is dead, Jack the Ripper died without revealing his awful secret.

AN OFT-ASKED QUESTION

Who was Jack the Ripper?

This question has often been asked since the days of the Whitechapel horrors, and there have been many criminologists who have maintained that Scotland Yard knew the truth, but kept it secret.

A number of eminent people have stated that Jack the Ripper was known to the police a few days after the Dorset Street murder, the most inhuman and insane of the whole series.

According to this solution, the Terror was a demented Russian doctor who had been haunting the East End for a number of years before the Buck's Row murder.

Living from hand to mouth, he got to know every court and alley in Whitechapel, and in fits of homicidal mania he murdered the unfortunate women whom he encountered in the dark. The mutilations were due to his frenzy at the sight of blood, and there were varying reasons given why he took away certain parts of the body.

After the Dorset Street affair his mind became completely unhinged and, fearing that the police were on his track, he jumped into the Thames near London Bridge and was drowned.

In the course of their usual inquiries into a case of suicide the police found in his room enough evidence to prove conclusively that he was Jack the Ripper.

Another explanation is that Jack the Ripper was a foreign Jew, a well-known character in the East End, but though the police had plenty of circumstantial evidence against him, they could never bring home his guilt and so he was not brought to trial.

Little heed need be paid to either of these solutions. The police knew nothing about Jack the Ripper.

Half a dozen persons were under suspicion but in every case, the evidence was of the very flimsiest, and a statement from any of the parties concerned would probably have established their innocence at once.

Nine women met their death in the Whitechapel area during the reign of terror and not once did the police really have a clue that was of any real value.

Jack the Ripper may well have been a mad doctor, but the police at that time knew nothing about him, and he certainly never committed suicide in the manner described.

**A typical Whitechapel market scene. It was round about this locality
that Jack the Ripper committed his crimes.**

At the period he is now said to have taken his life, the whole country was in a state of the wildest alarm. The crimes had caused great political consequences. The Chief Commissioner of Police resigned owing to the agitation against him. If the identity of Jack the Ripper had become known there was every reason why the facts should be revealed at once and so quieten the universal terror.

Instead, the police became more vigilant than ever and when Alice McKenzie was later found murdered in Castle Alley, the new Chief Commissioner personally supervised the operations designed to catch Jack the Ripper, directing special attention to the docks, which were kept under close observation for several years afterwards.

In the annals of Scotland Yard, no criminal has ever been the subject of so much secrecy as the silent Terror, but I for one, am only too well aware that the secrecy was designed to cover the official ignorance.

I have had the opportunity of studying most of the documents concerned with these crimes. Nearly one thousand statements were taken by the police, most of them vague and contradictory, and the number of inquiries they made must have been many times that number.

POLICE LEFT COMPLETELY BAFFLED

The police after a very bad start, did their best, but the swiftness and silence of Jack the Ripper left them baffled.

Yet we can only read the words with the feeling that the unknown murderer was exceptionally fortunate in never being detected. He took great risks and was lucky in never being seen properly by anyone in the districts where he carried out his crimes.

While his work pointed to the fact that he was a madman, yet he showed great cunning in all he did.

He knew Whitechapel thoroughly, otherwise he could never have got out of the maze of the alleys and courts after he had been interrupted when standing over the body of Alice McKenzie.

A great deal has been made of the fact that all his victims were women of a particular class, and significance is attached to the mutilations he made.

I do not think – nor did the police and medical men who were consulted all the time – that there was any special significance in his choice of victim.

They were the only class of women he could have persuaded to enter the dark spots where he murdered them, and it was in their own interest that they were anxious to shun passers-by and the police, and contributed to their own fate.

But in the case of Elizabeth Stride and Marie Kelly – neither of whom had fallen to the level of their companions – some special inducement must have been offered to get them to accompany the murderer. It will be remembered that Elizabeth Stride was not of the street-walking type, while Marie Kelly had never before taken a stranger to her house.

This inducement Scotland Yard believed to be either two or three sovereigns or else brightly polished coins which resembled gold.

POCKETS OF VICTIMS ALWAYS SEARCHED

When Alice McKenzie met her fate in Castle Alley, and Jack the Ripper had only a second or two in which to escape detection, two highly polished farthings were found near the body.

A short time before Annie Chapman met her death, a woman saw her with a foreign-looking man, who the previous evening, had tried to lure her into a darkened court by offering her two bright coins which turned out to be farthings.

In addition to this, a curious feature of the early discoveries was that the pockets of the victims had been searched and yet all the contents, including money, were left intact beside the body.

What was Jack the Ripper searching for? Nothing seemed more probable than that he took away the coins which he had given his victim, in case any clue would be left which might lead to his capture.

Having lured the women into the darkness, he acted with ferocious decision. The doctors, in their confidential reports, were of the opinion that he managed to get behind the women, and grasping the chin with the left hand, drew his knife across the throat to the right, resulting in a wound suggesting the work of a left-handed man who had attacked his victim from the front.

It is remarkable that in not one instance did his victims raise a cry for help. Death was practically instantaneous.

Why Jack the Ripper then mutilated them no one can tell. His actions suggest madness, but on this point it is of importance to observe that this type of crime had often before been practised on the Continent by men accounted sane.

INFERRED THAT HE WAS A FOREIGNER

From this fact the police inferred that he was a foreigner, backed as it was by the vague descriptions given of him on the two occasions when for a fleeting second, he had been glimpsed.

It is generally believed that Jack the Ripper had in his time been a doctor or medical student, otherwise he could never had accomplished his purpose in the short time generally at his disposal.

This was not, I may reveal, supported by the medical experts who were consulted at the time; on the contrary, they were definitely of the opinion that Jack the Ripper had no surgical experience, but that his handiwork showed he had a knowledge of anatomy, such as may have been gained by a slaughterer of animals.

Add to these conclusions the fact that he undoubtedly tracked in great caution – probably due to the use of rubbers on his boots – and that when he could, he carried away parts of the body, and you have practically all the definite facts that were of use to the police.

Again I must give the opinion of the doctors on the point that Jack the Ripper must have been bloodstained after every one of his crimes, and yet, if he was living in the East End, he never caused the slightest suspicion to his neighbours by his appearance.

The detectives were forced to the conclusion that either he did not live in the Whitechapel district, or else his acquain-tances were so used to seeing his every-day clothes stained in blood that they were never suspicious.

Very strict inquiries were made to determine if the Ripper was really a medical student or a mad doctor, and drawing a blank, Scotland Yard were strongly of the opinion that he was a cattleman.

In coming to this conclusion they were certainly assisted by some facts which came into their possession from a custom's officer. It concerned the suspicious behaviour of a certain cattleman whose boat arrived in the docks always a day or, at the most, two days before another murder was committed.

I have told how the police were organised to watch every cattle boat, but there is one fact left to relate which is very interesting.

After the murder of Marie Kelly, great astonishment was caused when a proclamation was issued offering a pardon to Jack the Ripper's accomplice if he turned Queen's Evidence.

Nobody thought for a minute that he really had an accomplice. The crimes of Jack the Ripper showed him to be absolutely inhuman. It was too much to think that there was yet another monster, equally inhuman, acting in concert with him.

Naturally it was thought when the offer of a pardon was issued that Scotland Yard had information on the point they did not wish to reveal.

The truth, I may state, is that there was not a single official who believed Jack the Ripper had an accomplice.

The proclamation was issued chiefly to deceive the suspected cattleman. Some detectives in making inquiries of the man had allowed their identity to become known and the proclamation was intended to reassure him and make him confident that the police were on the wrong track.

Whether he took fright or not, nobody ever knew, but on the next trip he left his boat unexpectedly and his trail was never picked up again.

The police had then the chance to connect him in the crime when Frances Coles met her fate, but the unfortunate incident when suspicion pointed so strongly to Sadler as the guilty man, induced them to stop their inquiries and a number of boats were enabled to leave the Thames without being searched.

Acquainted as I am with all the facts of the case, I cannot help but agree that the police acted on the most probable conclusion.

A cattleman from a foreign boat had opportunities of committing the murders such as no one else could avail themselves of, provided he knew Whitechapel intimately and there was not a doubt that the suspect had the necessary knowledge.

At night time he could leave his boat, carry out his crime and hasten back to his hiding place, without his appearance exciting the least wonderment. And in his knowledge of anatomy he knew enough and no more, to do what he set out to do.

It is a possible theory, no doubt the best that could be built up from the facts that were at the command of the police but even so it is only a theory.

Scotland Yard were always aware of this and no explanation of the crimes, however strange, could have surprised them.

INQUIRIES CONTINUED FOR YEARS

For many years afterwards inquiries were still made among pawnbrokers in the hope that Jack the Ripper would make a false step.

Only once, it will be recalled, did he rob a victim of any articles. From the fingers of Annie Chapman he tore two cheap rings, which in the dim light may have seemed of value.

There always remained the possibility that one day those rings might find their way into the hands of a pawnbroker in exchange for a few coppers, but Jack the Ripper, if he is still alive, alone can tell what happened to them.

One point remains to be dealt with. In all the accounts that have been published of those dark days, no mention has been made of four mysterious crimes which caused the Yard great anxiety.

In each case the dismembered remains of a young woman was found in London, and not only did they bear a striking similarity to one another, but in two of them the wounds and mutilations were practically identical with those inflicted on the Whitechapel victims.

Only one of these victims was identified and I mentioned earlier the case of the Pimlico girl, and the one definite conclusion that emerged from the police inquiries was that she had been the victim of a complete stranger just like the unfortunate women in the East End.

They were mysteries that baffled the police. The crimes stopped at the same time as the Whitechapel ones, and more than one official feared that there was a close connection.

OVER THREE HUNDRED CRIMES

Over three hundred crimes were committed throughout the country in this period by men whose minds had been affected by the horrors of Whitechapel, including 16 murders.

Such figures may convey better than words the ordeal which the people were called upon to undergo before they could once again breath freely.

James Sadler, who because of the chiming of a clock was saved from being found guilty of the last of the series of crimes, summed-up the matter in a way which the folk of the East End could well understand.

"They are a wonderful series of crimes," he said, half in bewilderment, half in queer admiration, "to study them is like studying the Bible, for you are as far off as ever when you've done."

It is unlikely that the mystery of Jack the Ripper, or the reason which drove him to his dark deeds, will ever be known.

He may yet be alive, an old man bowed down by awful and secret guilt. Time will have robbed him of his power for evil, and never again will women and children cower in fear at the mention of the name.

There is little chance of his like ever being known again.

Appendix:
Chapman Was Not Jack the Ripper

JACK THE RIPPER THEORY

I now come to one of the most singular developments in this case – the theory that George Chapman was no other than Jack the Ripper who had terrorised the East End of London in 1888 and 1889, by his series of murders of women of the unfortunate class.

This theory is no new one. I well remember the sensation it caused when it was first discussed in 1903, soon after the execution of Chapman.

Chief Inspector Abberline, who had been in charge of the investigations into the Ripper crimes, was positive that Chapman was the elusive murderer. Other highly-placed officials expressed the same view. The public, quick to see the similarity between the natures of the two criminals, were elated at the thought that the Ripper had been caught at last, and there were minor celebrations in the East End.

But after a little time, doubts began to be freely expressed concerning the theory, and it had almost been forgotten when it was recently revived, with additional facts to support it.

I made thorough inquiries at the time of Inspector Abberline's contention, and what I found is conclusive, as far as I am concerned. Recently discovered facts, however impressive they may seem after all these years, do not affect the mystery surrounding the identity of Jack the Ripper.

It is clear that Jack the Ripper took a fiendish delight in his crimes. He stood to gain nothing but the gratification of luring the unfortunate women into dark alleys where he could suddenly do them to death. The mutilations he inflicted on them added to the thrill that murder gave him.

George Chapman belonged to the same type. He poisoned his "wives" simply to gloat over their agony. In his own way, he cared more for Mrs Spink, Bessie Taylor and Maud Marsh than for any other women who came into his eventful life, yet he could watch them slowly dying without the slightest compunction.

COINCIDENCES

What was he doing in 1888 when London was in the grip of the Terror?

The answer is certainly startling.

He was employed as a barber's assistant, first in the Whitechapel Road and then in West India Dock Road, during the whole of that period. He lived mysteriously, seldom returning to his lodgings until between two and three in the morning.

He had come from Poland in the Spring of 1888, and though earning a living as a hairdresser, had spent three years as assistant to a surgeon in his native country. He understood something about anatomy, and Jack the Ripper, it will be remembered, almost certainly had similar knowledge.

Only once during the Ripper murders was a glimpse seen of the murderer in the

company of a victim. When Mary Kelly was done to death in her house in Miller's Court, the most revolting of the whole series of crimes, the police obtained a fairly accurate description of this suspect. They published it everywhere, and it ran: "Height 5ft. 4in., aged 34 or 35; dark complexion with moustache curled at ends."

Though Chapman was a much younger man than 35, the description fitted him perfectly, for he looked many years older than his age.

The suspect was noticed to be wearing many rings and a heavy gold watch chain. Chapman went about similarly bedecked.

When the hue and cry for the Ripper was at its height, two anonymous letters were handed to the police which showed that the writer knew more about the crimes than any of the detectives actually on the case.

One letter ran:

Dear Boss,

I keep on hearing that the police have caught me, but they won't fix me just yet. The joke about Leather Apron gave me real fits, and I shan't keep ripping till I do get buckled. Grand work, the last job was. I gave the lady no time to squeal.

I love my work and want to start again. Ha! ha! The next job I shall do I shall clip the lady's ears off and send them to the police, just for jolly, wouldn't you.

Jack the Ripper.

The second read:

I was not codding, dear old boss, when I gave you the tip. You'll hear about Saucy Jack's work to-morrow. Double event this time. Number one squealed a bit. Had not time to get ears for police. Thanks for keeping last letter back till I got to work again.

Jack the Ripper.

It has been pointed out that there are many Americanisms in these cards and that Chapman used similar expressions and passed himself off as an American. Also, the grim humour is very characteristic of the poisoner.

Even more curious is the fact that Chapman disappeared and settled down in New Jersey, U.S.A., directly after the Ripper murders had ceased. He was there for 18 months and during that time New Jersey was terrified by an outbreak of Ripper murders which ceased when Chapman returned to England.

Taking all these coincidences together it would appear as if a strong case had been made out for declaring Chapman to be Jack the Ripper, but under closer examination the whole fabric falls to pieces.

True, Chapman did come to England just before the East End was thrown into terror, and he lived a mysterious life. Extensive police enquiries were made to clear up this part of the affair, but owing to the number of years that had passed, it was quite impossible to discover what Chapman had been doing on the nights when the Whitechapel unfortunates were lured to their doom.

But from those who knew him in those days, there is the assurance that he kept largely to himself owing to the intrigues with various women that he was conducting even then. He behaved like a lady killer, making appointments nearly every night, and behaving very secretly about them.

His employer in the Whitechapel Road was positive that Chapman or Klosowski as he knew him, knew very little about the bad spots in Whitechapel in 1888. For Chapman, despite all his boasting, was a coward, and did not like to venture alone into the dark alleys of ill-repute where all the Ripper murders took place.

More important still, the woman with whom he lodged in the West India Dock Road was positive that he could not have committed the first of the Ripper crimes. That took place on the night of the August Bank Holiday in 1888, and she fixed the date easily because that night she gave a small party to a number of Poles, whom Chapman, who was new to the country and lonely, was anxious to meet.

Again, as far as is known, Chapman never associated with women of the unfortunate class. Even in his early days in London he was pursuing girls of respectable family, delighting in his conquests.

His papers showed him to possess medical knowledge. It is, however, more than doubtful if he had any knowledge of the use of the surgeon's knife. His training had consisted in attending Polish doctors who went in for the old-fashioned remedy of "blood-letting" in time of illness, and Chapman's duties were to be in attendance with necessary basins and towels. All the time he was in England he never once claimed to have surgical knowledge.

This is significant, for he was forever boasting of his skill in medicine, of which he had a smattering.

The description of the wanted Jack the Ripper certainly applied to him, but the same thing could be applied to thousands of others. Study it carefully, and recalling that in the 80's all men had curled moustaches, and were fond of displaying their rings and gold alberts, the idea of fixing on to one man is ludicrous.

ANONYMOUS LETTERS

When we come to consider the anonymous letters in the Ripper case, that particular link gives away at once. Firstly Chapman could not write fluent English at any stage of his career. Secondly, since at that time he had never been to America, how on earth could he have been responsible for the Americanisms? Not that I can distinguish them easily, for to me the letters are pure Cockney slang, and the humour is likewise the vulgar humour of the Cockney.

Finally, and to remove all doubt it was a simple matter for me to compare the handwriting of Chapman with that of the reproduced anonymous letters. There was no resemblance.

The coincidence of the New Jersey murders with Chapman's arrival is also without significance. His wife was with him in America, and stated that the murders occurred far away from where they were living, and her husband could not have been the guilty man.

But what about the Ripper crimes in Germany which occurred at the same time and which are identical with those in the East End? Chapman was certainly not in Germany, and it would be just as logical to brand him the Ripper if he had happened to be staying in Berlin.

I laid stress on the fact that similar crimes running into hundreds, were committed all over the world after the Whitechapel murders, and no matter to which country Chapman had gone, he would have been near the scene of some of them. To blame him for them is absurd.

There is still further indirect evidence to consider. One thing impressed both public and the police concerning Jack the Ripper and explained the terror he created. During the whole of his series of crimes he was never once heard. And it is more than doubtful if he was ever seen. He worked swiftly and silently, twice making his escape when apparently all avenue of escape had been cut off.

Now compare that with George Chapman, physically one of the clumsiest men. People who knew him well, told me that to see him running was a comical sight. While his wives were lying seriously ill he could never manage to tip-toe silently into the room, and he was forever apologising for the disturbance he caused. I simply cannot imagine such a man in the role of Jack the Ripper.

CHANGE OF METHODS

Is it possible that he landed in London a complete stranger and speaking no English, and within two months was engaged in his work with the knife, while showing an intimate knowledge of Whitechapel's dark spots which few men possessed?

Then, quite unaccountably, he ceases to murder and for eight years is content with flirting with women, before breaking out again. And in the second outbreak, to satisfy his cruel nature, he abandons a method which has proved conspicuously successful and adopts one which is quite the opposite in every respect. From swift killing with the

Chapman in the dock.

knife in the dark, he takes to slow poisoning in his own home.

Such a change in method by a murderer has never been recorded before, and it is impossible to believe that it happened in this case.

Chapman's early life in London was certainly mysterious, but there was no reason why the police should not have solved it. Before Chapman was executed, they could have approached him through his solicitor to ask for information concerning his Whitechapel days and given him the chance to meet accusations which were not made until after his death.

Nothing was done; no questions were asked. When, after Chapman's execution the plausible theory was put forward with every appearance of justification, it was eagerly seized upon, and it certainly brought relief to many a mother in the East End who still dreaded the re-appearance of the Terror.

The idea, however, was rejected by everyone who, like myself, made their own inquiries. There was not at that time, nor is there now, the least bit of direct evidence connecting Chapman with the Whitechapel murders. I think that it can be safely said that George Chapman, alias Severin Klosowski, was not Jack the Ripper.

Even so, he was one of the most notorious criminals this country has known. He was the passionate lover and supreme hypocrite who would feign grief over the sufferings of the women dying slowly at his hands; and his own fate was a merciful one compared to theirs. Thank goodness such men are rare.

R.J. Lees Again

By Stewart P. Evans

*We're honored to welcome **Stewart P. Evans** back to these pages. He is the co-author of several highly-regarded Ripper books and the author of* **Executioner: The Chronicles of James Berry, Victorian Hangman.**

One of the most enduring myths in the story of Jack the Ripper and the White-chapel Murders is that of the clairvoyant spiritualist R. J. Lees. Just when you thought that you had read everything on this tale, another item emerges to add to the biblio-graphy. The story of Lees and his alleged 'hunt for the Ripper' is too well known to need re-telling here, but slightly less well-publicised is the dismissal of the tale by Dr. Donald J. West, the then Research Officer

R.J. Lees, the star of a long-running myth about the Jack the Ripper case.

of the Society for Psychical Research (SPR) in 1949. His investigation of the Lees tale was published in the *Journal of the Society for Psychical Research,* London, Vol. XXXV, No. 653, July-August 1949. For the Lees believers West's report was 'devas-tating'. He demonstrated that the accounts were unreliable, investigated key points that were found to be distorted and even wrote to New Scotland Yard and the Home Office for the official 'take' on the business. Both denied any knowledge of, or possession of any documents relating to, Lees' escapades. Lees' story has been referred to many times over the years since it was fully detailed in the *Daily Express* of 7, 9, and 10 March 1931. The *Express* headline declared 'CLAIRVOYANT WHO TRACKED JACK THE RIPPER.' Sensational stuff, and the real birth of a legend that was not going to be dismissed easily.

Another pretty workmanlike and more deeply researched demolition of the absurd Lees story was conducted by author Melvin Harris in *The Unexplained* magazine in 1981 and in his books *Sorry, You've Been Duped!*, London, Weidenfeld and Nicolson, 1986, and *Jack the Ripper The Bloody Truth*, London, Columbus Books, 1987. It is quite a pastime to collect the many versions of the Lees tale and articles about it. It appears in many odd places and has been spotted in *Fate* magazine, *Answers, Light, Prediction, Criminologist,* and *Two Worlds.* And so the list goes on ... Of course, many

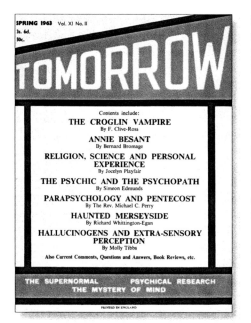

SPRING 1963 Vol. XI No. II
3s. 6d.
50c.

TOMORROW

Contents include:

THE CROGLIN VAMPIRE
By F. Clive-Ross

ANNIE BESANT
By Bernard Bromage

RELIGION, SCIENCE AND PERSONAL
EXPERIENCE
By Jocelyn Playfair

THE PSYCHIC AND THE PSYCHOPATH
By Simeon Edmunds

PARAPSYCHOLOGY AND PENTECOST
By The Rev. Michael C. Perry

HAUNTED MERSEYSIDE
By Richard Whittington-Egan

HALLUCINOGENS AND EXTRA-SENSORY
PERCEPTION
By Molly Tibbs

Also Current Comments, Questions and Answers, Book Reviews, etc.

THE SUPERNORMAL   PSYCHICAL RESEARCH
THE MYSTERY OF MIND

PRINTED IN ENGLAND

**The issue of *Tomorrow* magazine
with the article about the Lees legend.**

of the spiritualist versions uncritically accept the story, despite any debunking that may have taken place. The Lees legend has also migrated to film over the years, Lees making an excellent character to spice up the storyline. There is no doubt that there is room for a complete book thoroughly investigating the whole story and its development. *The Lees Ripper Legend* would make an excellent title.

I suppose, then, that I should not be surprised to find even more 'new' pieces on this aspect of Ripper lore. Recently I was having lunch with members of the Ghost Club in a remote Essex pub, when I was approached by the Ghost Club Chairman Alan Murdie. Alan showed me a rare magazine he had recently discovered in the collection of our late mutual friend, distinguished author and investigator Andrew Green. Alan's query was about an article in the magazine called 'Haunted Merseyside' and written by my friend Richard Whit-

tington-Egan. Noticing that the magazine contained several other articles of more than passing interest, I asked Alan if I could browse through it over lunch. He agreed, and I began to read. The magazine was *Tomorrow,* Spring 1963, Vol. XI No. II, published in London and edited by F. Clive-Ross. I came to an essay on page 132 with the title 'The Psychic and the Psychopath' by Simeon Edmunds, associate editor of the magazine. I was amazed to find that it was all about Dr. West's 1949 SPR investigation of the Lees' story.

It was an interesting and quite well researched piece briefly looking at the murders and including the 'saucy Jacky' postcard and the 'Lusk letter'. The 'famous spiritualist medium' Lees was discussed and his Ripper story told again, including the 'well-known doctor' and the subsequent 'fake funeral' and the burial of an 'empty coffin'. Simeon Edmunds concluded the account of the story with the words –

> And there, for many years, the matter rested. The account, however often it was retold and rehashed, always made a good story. Dismissed, of course, by the sceptics, it was, nevertheless, accepted by many as factual, while the supporters of spiritualism not unnaturally acclaimed it as supporting their belief in the powers of mediums. Nothing, however, seems to have been done to check the authenticity of the story until 1948, when Dr. Donald J. West, then Research Officer of the Society for Psychical Research, began a systematic and thorough inquiry. Alas for believers, his report was devastating...

The details of Dr. West's report were then given and endorsed by the writer. It finished –

The conclusion then must be that this story, like others beloved of many spiritualists and believers in the "occult," does not stand up to serious, impartial investigation. In the words of Dr. West, "the claim that the medium Lees helped to trace 'Jack the Ripper' is not supported by the known facts. Scotland Yard denies all knowledge of the medium, and no one can be found to fit the description of the mad doctor who was supposed to have disappeared."

This piece ran a full three pages and was previously unknown to me. I remarked to Alan that here was another Ripper item missing from the bibliographies and he replied, 'Oh yes, I forgot to mention that.'!

In doing some follow-up research on the Edmunds' essay I discovered that a Lees' supporter was not long in responding to the critique. In the summer 1963 issue of *Tomorrow* a letter appeared in the correspondence section of the magazine. It was dated 'Aberdeen 24.4.63' and headed 'R.J. Lees and the Ripper'. The writer, a certain C. Nelson Stewart commenced –

Sir,- Having delved in the Ripper mystery at various times, and also pondered the story of the intervention by R.J. Lees, I was much interested in Mr. Simeon Edmunds' article .... Assuming that the main arguments put forward by Dr. West have been summarized in the article, I still feel that the question remains open ...

Well, they do say it's hard to keep a good legend down. The correspondent, a former civil servant, pointed out, from experience, how official organizations, such as the police and the Home Office, find it easy 'to give the official lie without technically putting down an untruth.' He had

been in touch with veteran Ripper author Donald McCormick who told him that he had attempted to identify 'the psychotic physician' when researching for his book, *The Identity of Jack the Ripper* (1959). It was possible that no obituary notice may have been printed 'in the anxiety to stifle the whole matter, or to avoid legal complications.' Mr. Stewart pointed out cases where official documents had 'disappeared' in the past and where mention was missing in contemporary journals, letters or biographies. The Aberdeen correspondent summed up, "Dr. West cannot say in this instance that the 'known facts' as a result of his inquiries show that the whole thing was a myth." And, "But it certainly shows the naivete of Dr. West in treating the public prints as reliable scientific data."

In reply to this letter, Simeon Edmunds commented –

The point that Mr. Stewart seems to have overlooked is that no good evidence appears to exist for believing the R.J. Lees story. In the absence of such evidence, Dr. West's interpretation is surely the reasonable one. Mr. Stewart has overlooked or ignored also the fact that the police were still arresting suspects long after the date of Jack the Ripper's last crime.

So the Ripper commentators were at it way back in the early '60s arguing the toss over interpretations and, no doubt, opening themselves up to accusations of a 'personal attack'. It seems that not much changes.

As for me, well, the most interesting piece in the magazine was a detailed investigation of a story I had first read when I was about 11 years old. It was a story titled 'The Croglin Vampire' – now *there's* a real legend and mystery worthy of deeper research!

Ghost Club Presents:
A Day With Jack

By Jennifer Pegg

*In November of last year **Ripper Notes** columnist **Jennifer Pegg** made the trip to London to attend a conference about Jack the Ripper that was hosted by the Ghost Club. Here's what she had to say about the event.*

Ever wondered what happens when you fill a room with a bunch of Ripper buffs and an organization of ghost hunters? The result was a thoroughly enjoyable atmosphere and an interesting set of seminars on the paranormal and Jack which I am sure were of interest to both sets of enthusiasts. The event was organised by Ghost Club council member and Ripper enthusiast Philip Hutchinson, who may be a familiar name to readers of *Ripper Notes* as he doubles as a London tour guide.

The first seminar of the day was 'The Springheeled Jack Attacks Of 1838', which was delivered by Alan Murdie, the Chairman of the Ghost Club. This was an interesting and informative presentation, especially for me as I have to confess to having never heard of the Springheeled Jack hysteria before this point. The stories, it seems, grew out of fact but soon turned to myth. Springheeled Jack sightings were reported all over the country, with the mysterious figure jumping over hedges and generally scaring people for nearly forty years. Mr Murdie drew comparisons to Jack the Ripper throughout his presentation. He also pointed out that there were relatively few books and source material on the Springheeled Jack attacks. In fact there are only two main sources, and I'm sure you won't be surprised to learn that they were in disagreement on many points. So comparisons with Ripperology *spring* to mind (sorry for the pun there).

The second seminar of the day was 'The History of Jack the Ripper', presented by Stewart P. Evans. Now, I bet you are thinking, *What was that about? Jack the*

Ripper? Never heard of him! Right? Well, this was an introduction to the case mainly for the benefit of the people in attendance who were not already Ripper enthusiasts. They may well have had no clue what the rest of the seminars were about without it, but I am sure they had a lot clearer understanding after this talk. In fact it is hard to imagine there could be a better introduction to the case than one from Stewart (he can pay me for that endoresement later). It was thoroughly entertaining even if you knew about Jack, as I am sure the rest of the Ripper folk there would testify. As you would expect from Stewart, the account provided was enjoyable and comprehensive, packed with information. He presented a slide show with pictures covering many aspects of the case. Stewart took questions at the end of his seminar. Naturally he was asked some inevitable questions by some Ghost Club members about whether James Maybrick or Walter Sickert was the Ripper, but these were dealt with firmly and politely in a way that hopefully made it clear that they are not considered to be serious suspects.

The next speaker was Stephen Butt who spoke about 'Robert James Lees and the Psychic Hunt For Jack the Ripper'. This seminar was about some whether the story that Robert Lees tracked down the Whitechapel murderer using his psychic abilities was correct or not. Stephen explained that a lot of the story is based upon distorted information and, as such, must be taken with a grain of salt. I must confess that this particular topic was my primary reason for attending the event. It was quite worthwhile, as I quite thoroughly enjoyed it.

The whole day was rounded off by the last speaker, Philip Hutchinson, who presented a seminar titled 'The Ghosts of Jack the Ripper'. This was a lively and enthusiastic talk which provided an overview of the reports of spirits-from-beyond related to the case in some way. A vast array of ghost stories have built up around the case, as you might expect considering the tabloid nature of the crimes. The souls of the Ripper victims get around a bit, or at least so it appeared from the many tales of ghostly hauntings and visitations that exist. There were, as you might expect, more reports concerning Mary Jane Kelly's spirit than the other victims. Many of these stories were not considered believable by Mr Hutchinson, which surprised me and taught me that I don't know a lot about ghost hunting! Mr Hutchinson also reviewed Pamela Ball's *Jack the Ripper A Psychic Investigation* and Jeanette Han's *Death Of A Prince* (incidentally, both books as well as the Robert Lees story were featured in an article by Wolf Vanderlinden in the previous issue of *Ripper Notes*). These books dealt with a paranormal search for the Ripper in modern times by their authors. To say he was not impressed by either one would be an understatement.

Hutchinson's lively and energetic talk rounded off a thoroughly enjoyable day. The organisers, who informed us that they had been trying to arrange the event for quite some time, deserve a lot of credit for hosting this one day conference. With any luck they will hold another in the future.

Moving?

Make sure your subscription to *Ripper Notes* follows you when you change your address. You can email your new shipping address to **dan@norder.com** or contact us by mail at one of the postal addresses listed on the first page of this issue.

A Cloak & Dagger Club Christmas

By Caroline Morris

*Caroline Morris is co-author with Seth Linder and Keith Skinner of **Ripper Diary - The Inside Story,** which was published by Sutton in 2003. She has been a regular contributor to the Casebook message boards since 1999, and occasionally writes reviews and articles for both **Ripper Notes** and **Ripperologist.***

Hello readers, Carrotty Nell speaking. I'm afraid I had to step in at the last minute to write about the tenth anniversary Christmas Spectacular held at the Cloak & Dagger Club in London's East End on Saturday December 4th. Caz was given the job but was so tipsy by nine o'clock that remembering her own name would have been a challenge. Women these days can't take the gin like we used to. So it falls to me, real name in life Frances Coles, the last of the Whitechapel victims, to do the ghost writing.

I always trot along to the Princess Alice on Commercial Street to see the gang coming home. They come from near and far and meet up every other month to talk about the old days in the old town. Of course the place is not the same as I remember it, 113 years ago before I was cruelly done in on the 13th day of February, missing out on all my Valentine cards. Even the boozer is now called the City Darts, as if I needed reminding that romance died with me.

It was fortunate that this former 'unfortunate' was there on Saturday, as per usual, with me sprig of holly on me bonnet. (Well, I thought they might appreciate a little festive spirit.) It amuses me to hear what the gang have to say about all the 'orrible murders that blighted what should have been the best years of a girl's life. I could tell 'em whether it was Jack, or Jim Sadler, or just another sad john, who witnessed my last moments in the flesh. And naturally I found out all there is to know about the real Ripper when we were finally reunited. But would

Alan Sharp and Caroline Morris in costume for the party.

All photos ©2004 by Alan Sharp

any of the gang hear me if I spilled the beans? And if they did, would they thank me for putting them out of their misery, or curse me for spoiling a good mystery? I better stick to describing the events of Saturday night.

It was unseasonably mild, as I wafted my way along Commercial, through the wall of the Darts, and up the apples and pears to where the action was. So mild it was that I could not raise the faintest chill in the place to cool the red cheeks of the silly devils arriving in costume. Coral Kelly was there, as always, to greet the living; Alan Sharp, a sharply dressed Gentleman Jack, followed the ladies with steely glint of eye (and knife too, given half a chance). One such lady, Liza Hopkinson, her eye blacked by a long-dead punter, soldiered on with petticoats swirling, to sell over two hundred quids-worth of raffle tickets to keep the club in funds over the coming year.

I didn't know whether to feel relief or cold panic when a series of shrill police whistles pierced through the laughter and chin wagging, stopping everyone dead in their tracks. But I knew my mince pies must be deceiving me when the source of all that whistling presented themselves for inspection: would you Adam 'n' Eve it? The two daft bloodhounds who couldn't catch a cold, never mind the cut-throat who caused such havoc back in 1888, had come back as none other than Adam Wood and Andy Aliffe! I felt quite faint – even more so than usual –

to see Barnaby and Burgho back on the Ripper's trail, and dressed up like coppers, if you please!

At this point in the proceedings, I was hovering above Robert Smith, done up like a dapper doctor. I thought he must have seen me go a whiter shade of pale, because he took from his pocket a small round box labelled "smelling salts", at the very moment I needed them most. But damn it, the box was empty. What a quack, and no black bag in sight! I was instantly back in Swallow Gardens, left to fend for myself, unseen and unheard by a living soul...

But within moments I was mercifully coaxed back to the present by the lovely Lindsay Siviter, modelling the limited edition Cloak & Dagger T-shirt – "where legend becomes history" – brought along by Frogg Moody. A quick twirl from Lindsay revealed the names of every guest speaker since the club was founded in 1994.

We were then treated to Mastermind

Left: Liza Hopkinson and Caroline Morris as a couple of tarts.
Right: Police bloodhounds Barnaby and Burgho (Adam Wood and Andy Aliffe) on the case.

The mastermind contest, from left to right: Adrian Morris, Frogg Moody, Andy Aliffe, Robert Ives, Sue Parry and Robert Clack.

meets Jack the Ripper. The winners of the first four raffle tickets drawn could gamble their prize for the chance to win the quiz. First contestant in the hot seat was long-standing club member Robert Ives (who was at school with Caz until the age of eleven). Next to face the quizmaster was Sue Parry, teacher-cum-lady of the night, looking very fetching in corset, bloomers and straw hat. Then came Rob Clack, who often walks the East End streets with me (although he doesn't know it) taking photographs and noting, as I do, the many changes to the old place. These three contenders managed to answer all their questions correctly (don't ask me what some barrister called Druitt, or the dear old Queen's doc, Sir William Gull, were doing in a quiz about the Whitechapel Murders), so it fell upon Frogg, the final brave soul, to match their score, and match it he did.

The first to answer the tie-breaker question correctly was Sue, who was duly declared the winner and awarded her prize, although no one went away empty-handed. I don't mind all this jollity; after all, nothing can hurt me like 'he' did. I do turn in me grave every time a new theory comes along – more theories than they've had hot

dinners, which is another sore point. There they were, tucking into their festive finger buffet, winning prize after prize in the raffle (several tens of prizes up for grabs, by my reckoning, including a Victorian sixpence or two), while I looked on, empty as ever. Just one more crust in me belly at the right time, or a shiny new sixpence in me pocket, might have saved me from the streets on that fateful night.

It would have warmed the cockles of poor Mary's missing heart to see Mick Warboys playing Father Christmas, bushy beard grown specially for the occasion, hearty laugh a permanent feature. But the sight of each raffle winner sitting on Mick's generous lap, having their image taken by a police dog with a camera, is one that will haunt me well into the New Year, I can tell you. I might get my own back, when the results of the club photo shoot are revealed. If there is an extra female shape that no one remembers seeing that night, don't be shocked; you can be sure I dress that way at every meeting, not just at Yuletide.

As for Caz, who had the nerve to begin life on the day mine was ended (well, no, not in the year 1891, admittedly, though she's no spring chicken), I had to sober her up quick when her number was drawn out. The prize she chose was a year's free subscription to this very periodical. She may get herself all dolled up like an 'unfortunate' on the first Saturday of each December, but unfortunate she ain't!

There is a rather fitting finale to my spirited Christmas story. I heard it said that the club may be on the move, as the City Darts is being sold shortly. Under new management, who knows if they would still be able to gather there in the coming months and years? How could I bear it if my precious gang could no longer join me in my favourite haunt? I had work to do.

On the Sunday morning, I tripped along behind Caz and her family, as they left the Darts. I know their custom is to walk along Wentworth Street, east in the direction of Brick Lane or west towards Petticoat Lane, to look for bargains in the markets. But that would not have served my purpose on this occasion.

So I blew them gently on up Commercial Street, and only stopped blowing when the party reached the Golden Heart. My own heart skipped a beat as they hesitated by the door, then gladdened as they pushed it open and went inside for the first time in their lives.

A cheery fire and the even cheerier landlady greeted us, and drinks were ordered. Before you could say Jack the Ripper, Caz was telling the landlady about the previous night, just as I hoped she would. And no sooner did she mention the worries over where the Cloak & Dagger Club's future lay, than a piece of paper was pressed into her hand, bearing the name and telephone number of the landlady's son, who is taking over the City Darts. A final whisper from Carrotty Nell and the charm was wound up: Caz did the suggesting for me. "Would your son consider changing the pub's name back to the Princess Alice?" "Oh yes", came the reply. "He is planning to do just that."

So maybe, just maybe, I'll see the gang

Raffle-winner Loretta Lay sits on the knee of Santa Claus (Mick Warboys) .

there as usual on the first Saturday of February, and some day soon I may see the old name restored. In the meantime, if you happen to be walking along Commercial Street, you won't see me, but you might just feel the chill wind and hear the rustle of many layers as I pass by.

February still makes me shiver. But then it always did.

For more details about the Cloak & Dagger Club, please contact:

Coral Kelly
170 Eswyn Road
Tooting
London
SW17 8TN
Coralkelly52@hotmail.com

Or visit the website at:
www.cloakanddaggerclub.org.uk

From the Newspaper Morgue
A look at the case as seen by contemporary news media

By Wolf Vanderlinden

This is the first segment of a new regular feature here at *Ripper Notes:* an in-depth look at some of the news stories that may shed more light on the Whitechapel murders. It is hoped that you the reader will find the articles instructive, entertaining or at least vaguely interesting. Some segments will present unrelated news reports while others, like this first offering, will revolve around a theme.

This issue's theme is:

Jack the Ripper Comes to North America? (Part 1)

In our last issue of *Ripper Notes* we printed a fascinating piece by Roger Peterson titled "Did Jack the Ripper Visit Leadville?" At the heart of this article was a letter received in 1889 by the marshal of the town of Leadville, Colorado, which was purportedly sent by London's Jack the Ripper.

This was not the first time that news of the Ripper's arrival in North America was reported to a panicky public, nor was it the first hoax letter received by an American or Canadian citizen. It got me thinking that other examples of this phenomenon might make an interesting start to "From the Newspaper Morgue," and as I have semi-godlike powers here at the magazine (Dan, of course, has the full godlike package) I have made it so.

The earliest mention of the Ripper's possible arrival in North America that I have found so far was reported by several New York area newspapers. Here is one example:

The *Brooklyn Eagle,*
10 November, 1888

London's Reign of Terror

The assassin of Whitechapel has claimed his ninth victim,[1] having planned and executed his latest crime with all the deliberation and cunning that characterized his former exploits. The record of these murders is one of the most startling in the criminal history of any country and while many theories have been advanced bearing on the identity of the culprit, no progress whatever has been made in the work of running him to ground. It is idle to blame the police and to institute comparisons between the efficiency of Scotland yard and that of the detective talent of New York. According to the last census London had a population of 5,500,000. There is but one policeman to every 625 people.[2] New York's police force, in proportion to population, is very much larger, and beside this, as superintendent Murray points out, our chief city has no locality that in misery and crime corresponds with the Whitechapel district.[3] The common assumption is that all the murders have been committed by the same person, and yet there would be no cause for surprise if it were discovered that such was not the case. However this may be, there is certainly great danger that the murders will appeal to disordered minds in other cities, and thus breed a spirit of slaughter horrible to contemplate. Already it is thought in some quarters that the fiend is likely to turn up anywhere. The mysterious disappearance of a woman named Caroline Rose from the steamer *Egypt* of the National Line during the vessel's last trip west is attributed to the Whitechapel murderer because a knife smeared with blood was found in her berth. All the steerage passengers, according to the morning papers, were inclined to think that "Jack the Ripper" had been aboard.[4]

The danger of imitation being duly considered, the fact remains that the probabilities favor a recurrence of the crime in the same part of London. The series of fifteen butcheries, which the monster is said to contemplate, is still far from complete.[5] Assuredly of great significance is it that all the victims belong to the same class of unfortunate women, for if the gratification of a homicidal mania was the sole thing in view the sex and character of the stricken would presumably not be the same in all instances. Rather there would be reason to infer that a variety of selections would be shown – that men, women and children from different walks of life would succumb to the assassin's knife. Something more, then, than ordinary bloodthirstiness must be premised, and, this admitted, the theory that the criminal is a reformatory maniac skilled in the use of the knife, cunning in the extreme, and probably perfectly sane on all other matters would appear to be the most tangible. It has been said among other things that the assassin is an American, because he wears a slouch hat. If so ghastly a series of tragedies may be said to possess an element of humor, it is in imputing the crimes to an American for the reason specified.[6] Much more reasonable would it be to infer that the murderer is a member or ex-member of the London police force, who, for some wrong, real or fancied, seeks to bring ridicule and disgrace on the entire police machinery of the metropolis.[7] In the absence of a more rational explanation we prefer to hold to the theory that the murderer believes he has a sublime moral mission to perform in the extermination of fallen women, and that it is by no means improbable that the butcheries are the result of a conspiracy of similarly affected fanatics.

It is difficult to exaggerate the alarm which the horrors have caused London. Here is the spectacle of a man killing at will, taking the keenest delight in his ability to evade detection and defying all the resources of civilization in his ghastly carnival. He mocks the detective skill of the proudest city in the world, and calmly announces that when his list of victims is complete he will gladly surrender. If there could be anything better calculated to bring into relief barreness [sic] of ingenuity and resource not only on the part of the officials but of the whole people, it is not easy to imagine. Not too much is it to say that one more victim, in view of the excited condition of the public mind in England, may have serious effect on the stability of the Ministry. However unreasonable and unjust it may be the complaint against the Salisbury administration on the score of its inability to catch the murderer is so bitter that there will be no cause for surprise if it were compelled to retire in contempt beneath the lash of general condemnation. It is time for action, and the authorities of London can now well afford to turn the city upside down in their endeavours to allay popular clamor.

Notes on this article:

1) There seems to have been no consensus amongst the news media as to how many victims the Ripper had claimed by this point in time. The *Eagle* is following several newspapers in declaring nine: the "canonical" five; the Whitehall torso; Martha Tabram; Emma Smith and the fictional unnamed woman who later became known as "Fairy Fay." Other papers chose eight, dropping "Fairy Fay." The more reliable London papers, such as the *Times* and the *Daily*

Telegraph, reported seven: the "canonical" five; Martha Tabram and Emma Smith.

2) The *Brooklyn Eagle* has taken this figure from a *New York Times* article published on the same day titled "London's Small Police Force". The figure is incorrect. In 1888 the ratio, given all ranks, was more like 1 policeman to every 385 people for the city of London. New York City, with a population of roughly 1,3000,000 and with a police force of 3200 men, had, at 1 policeman for every 406 people, a slightly worse ratio. Another example of the New York area papers attempting to make their own police force look superior to those of London.

3) This is in regards to an interview Murray gave the day before and which was reported in *The New York Sun* also on the 10th of November, 1888. It is hard to believe that Murray actually believed this to be true considering hellish New York slums such as Five Points, the Fourth Ward, Hell's Kitchen and the Tenderloin. It's especially unlikely considering the fact that Murray had been a Precinct Captain in the Fourth Ward for several years, at a time when it was deservedly known as the "Bloody Fourth."

4) The reason why I chose this article: the "mysterious disappearance" from the steamship *Egypt* of Caroline Rose who went missing from the ship while en route from Liverpool to New York. The finding of the blood smeared knife makes it obvious why the steerage passengers believed that she was another Ripper victim and therefore that Jack had arrived in North America. This belief seems rooted in a panic reminiscent of fear of ships carrying plague. Who knew if some steamer might not bring the Ripper across the Atlantic undetected like some malignant disease allowing him to flit amongst an unsuspecting American populace like the Red Death gliding amongst

Prince Prospero's guests.

Even more interesting is the ship on which this tragedy occurred. The *S.S. Egypt* was part of the National Steam Navigation Company, or National Line, which ran a dozen vessels between Britain and the Port of New York. Interesting because Michael Conlon's Ripper suspect, Arbie La Bruckman, worked as a butcher/cattleman on the ships of the National Line. Is this one more piece of evidence that points to La Bruckman's guilt? Only if La Bruckman hadn't murdered Mary Kelly, as the *Egypt* arrived in New York on the same day that Kelly was butchered in London.

5) After the Annie Chapman murder several newspapers reported that a message was left at the scene at No. 29 Hanbury Street. The *Daily Telegraph,* 10 September, 1888, pointing out that there was absolutely no corroboration for this, stated that the words, *"I have done three, and intend to do nine more and give myself up,"* were reported by some to have been found written on a wall in Hanbury Street. This newspaper also offered an alternate version, *"Five - fifteen more and I give myself up,"* supposedly written on a piece of paper found in the backyard where the murder took place. In all likelihood these messages are garbled references to blood stains reportedly found on a wall of No. 25 Hanbury Street and a blood soaked piece of paper supposedly found in the yard abutting the end of No. 25. In actual fact the blood on the wall turned out to be urine stains while, according to Inspector Chandler, no bloody paper was found anywhere.

6) Various pieces of "evidence" seemed to point to an American. Among them: "Americanisms" found in the Dear Boss letter; Coroner Baxter's American doctor supposedly attempting to buy uteri; the possibility that Texas cowboys or Native Americans were responsible, and the Irish/

American suspect Dr. Francis Tumblety. The "slouch hat" mentioned here is probably a reference to the "wide awake" hat (a large stiff brimmed hat similar to the large floppy brimmed slouch hat) supposedly worn by a man Matthew Packer claimed he saw with Elizabeth Stride on the night of her murder. The *Daily Telegraph,* 6 October, 1888, described this hat as a *"soft felt or American hat."* Evan the Scotland Yard files record this hat as being a *"kind of Yankee hat."* Packer's description is preceded, however, by the arrest of a suspect on 30 September (see the *Times,* 1 October, 1888) at a Union Street lodging house who was wearing an "American hat." It is possible that Packer incorporated this description into his story.

7) An early "policeman as suspect" theory. Although suspicion was thrown on Sergeant Thick by a member of the public in a letter sent to the Home Office on 10 September, 1889, the policeman as killer theory was made famous by Thomas Burke's fictional short story "The Hands of Mr. Ottermole" published in *The Pleasantries of Old Quong,* Constable, 1931. The *Eagle* theory neatly offers both a motive and an explanation for the murderer remaining uncaught but then downplays this by favouring the religious, or reforming, murderer or conspiracy of murderers.

So whatever happened to the theory of Caroline Rose, Ripper victim? Well, perhaps this article, which appeared on the same day as the *Eagle*'s, will begin to clear things up:

The *New York Times*
10 November, 1888

The Captain of the steamship Egypt, which arrived yesterday, reports that a steerage passenger named Caroline Rose was missing since the morning of Oct. 28,[1]

and it is supposed that she committed suicide by jumping overboard.

1) The *S.S. Egypt* left Liverpool on the 26th of October, so she was only a day and a half out when Caroline Rose disappeared.

That story of was followed the next day by a report refuting the theory that Rose was a Ripper victim:

The *New York Times*
11 November, 1888

IT WAS A CASE OF SUICIDE

The report that there had been foul play in the case of Mrs. Caroline Rose, whose suicide from the steamship Egypt was mentioned in yesterday's Times, was declared to be absolutely without foundation by the officers of the ship yesterday. It is quite evident from affidavits made by the passengers who were near the unfortunate woman's quarters that she was crazed by drink and had quietly jumped overboard after trying to stab herself with a knife.

So, a likely case of suicide. This is an early example of the death of a woman being attributed to the Whitechapel murderer without any evidence to support the theory other than a knife being involved in some way. On the other hand, since no body was ever found we cannot know for certain if Caroline Rose actually committed suicide or if she was murdered. But then, even if she were, there is no proof that points to Jack the Ripper being the likely suspect. On the contrary there is evidence, the murder of Mary Kelly on the 9th of November, 1888, which would tend to disprove it.

Next issue: Part two of "Jack the Ripper Comes to North America?" in which Jack surrenders to Canadian police and confesses all!

The Inquest

By Jennifer Pegg

This is the section of the magazine where you can weigh in with your opinions on specific topics related to the case. Don't forget to get involved. This issue's six questions focused on the field of Ripperology itself: what got us interested, what we hope to gain, what we should be doing. Thanks to everyone who took part.

Here are your responses:-

Question 1: How did you first become interested in the Jack the Ripper case?

Looking at the question above I find myself asking if I was just being nosey. But no there was a point. I have always been fascinated as to how people get involved in the field of Ripperology. I am sure I have bored you all before with my accidental discovery of books in the library story! It seems however, that accidental stumbling is the predominant way to discover the case. Though I hear they are doing it in schools now. (Why couldn't we have studied it when I was at school?)

"After having seen *From Hell* with Johnny Depp. I spent all the night on **www.casebook.org** to learn something about the Whitechapel Murders!"

"I saw a TV program which mentioned the production of *Jekyll and Hyde* that had to be cancelled because of the Jack the Ripper scare. Prior to that I'm not sure I even realised that Jack the Ripper was a real person. The next day I was in a bookstore and saw a copy of the 'Diary' – it is not something I would have normally looked at, but I picked it up and started reading it and have been hooked ever since."

"I learnt about Jack after reading a few books on the topic."

"When I was about 13 or 14 I read my older brother's copy of Don Rumbelow's book. I honestly can't remember what prompted the interest, probably just that passing ghoulish interest all young boys have in anything a bit shocking or gory. Let's face it, most small boy's favourite hobby is pulling the legs of insects, this is all just an extension of that."

"Upon reading a condensed version of Donald Rumbelow's *The Complete Jack the Ripper* which appeared in *Reader's Digest* magazine in perhaps 1975, I then went in search of the entire book, subsequently purchasing the 1976 Signet paperback edition, which I studied cover to cover. I've been hooked ever since."

"I became 'seriously' interested after discovering almost all I had previously assumed was true about the Whitechapel Murders was erroneous... The photograph of

MJK made – and still does have – an impact on me."

"I have always been interested in unsolved murder mysteries and Victorian history so it was only natural that I would drift into the case, which at times can be an obsession."

"I first became interested when I read the old *The Book of Lists* (Wallechinsky and Wallace) and saw some entries on the Ripper that sounded really bizarre. Only later did I discover that nearly everything in it, and especially the Ripper information, was completely unreliable."

I guess this goes to show books and films can lead to greater and better things!

Question 2: Do you think any theory as to the identity of Jack the Ripper can ever now be proved conclusively?

As we know, Ripperology is a diverse field. However, it can be strongly argued that one of our central issues is surely the identity of the infamous killer. So it was with this in mind I decided to ask for your opinions on whether or not his identity can be proved conclusively today. Here's what you had to say:-

"I think it's possible there may be information out there that could prove a case, but if there is we sure haven't found it yet."

"No. What could possibly prove that? A written confession? The Maybrick diary has proven we cannot rely on science to put the age and authenticity of a document beyond doubt, so even if a 'confession' was found and the Ripper wrote it, there would always still be those who question its credentials. People won't give up their own pet theories so easily."

"If I was being honest with myself I would have to answer no. How can we ever be sure that we are right? Only if we had a time machine could we actually be sure and sadly that seems to be a long way off."

"No. I think that some theories are better and more probable than others, but none of them is conclusive"

"My head tells me that the case will never be conclusively proven, but I hate to say no because there continue to be advances in the forensic sciences. Just think how much has changed in the last 10 years. There is also the outstanding research that continues to be completed by writers and enthusiasts around the world. Who knows what might be discovered that could be corroborated by additional evidence or something already in the historical record."

"Maybe if there were some definite piece of evidence lying around – but then again what are the chances of that!"

"To do that, we would need iron clad and irrefutable evidence to make the theory conclusive... that's a hard one to answer."

"Although the probability is very tiny, it exists, and provides the incentive for continued research."

"I doubt it, but the impossible has been known to happen."

I see you share my pessimism! Well, the majority of you anyway.

Question 3: Aside from the killer's identity, what other piece of information would you most like to know in relation to the Whitechapel Murders?

The big question might be easier to answer if we could have the information that would solve the smaller questions. So here's what you wanted to know:-

"I'd like to know which victims were killed by the same hand, and which were murdered independently."

"How many victims was JTR actually responsible for, who were the actual victims, was he active before and after the Whitechapel series."

"I would love to know the names of everyone he ever killed, since I suspect the list would hold some major surprises."

"I would always like to be sure of issues relating to some of the myths that have built up. For example I would want to know what was at Annie Chapman's feet. It might not lead to the killer but it would clear up a big point of uncertainty."

"If Jack killed Martha Tabram."

"If others may have known of his crimes and if so, were they intimidated in some way from disclosing information that may have prevented all of the canonical five murders, enabled capture, and clarified identity."

"Mary Kelly's complete history."

"Just who the hell was Mary Jane Kelly, where were her family? Who were her family? She is probably one of the most famous murder victims of all time, yet all we know is a name and a story attached to a corpse, both of which could well be entirely false. Why did some people allegedly know her as Emma? Are we looking for Mary Jane Kelly when we should be looking for Emma Davies? Or Davis? Why was she described as a tall, short, stout, dark haired, blonde red-head, who lived upstairs with the two children she didn't have? Did she really have such remarkably recognisable ears?"

Question 4: Do you think that Ripperology pays enough respect to the victims of Jack the Ripper?

One of things that is sometimes used against us (naming no names here) is that we do not give enough respect to the victims of Jack the Ripper or that we somehow overlook them as people. I just wondered if this was a fair point!

"I think Ripperology overall is pretty good at turning them into real people instead of caricatures, but there are a few authors and people outside of the field who have no respect for anyone, the victims included."

"Yes I do. It keeps their memory alive and shows them to be more than just a bunch of murdered unfortunates. Flowers are still placed on their graves, and they are remembered not only as victims but as women who lived in very difficult times."

"The 'walk-on' who visits Casebook or JTR Forums could spend weeks reading material and discussion on any of the 100 plus suspects and assume there is an inordinate amount of attention paid to these characters. However, those of us who do participate regularly in said discussions know better... The efforts in researching the case and the entire periphery, whether it's conditions in factories, occult and secret societies in London, quality of milk, or popular songs of that era, are important by-products of this case being studied to the extent that it is.... Who would have imagined a cadre of proletarian women, no more than a dozen, would have launched the scholarship that they did? The women, in a morbid sense, can't be repaid enough for this fact... but in other ways they are being given their due."

"It's probably fair to say that far more time is spent trying to catch the killer than learn about the victims, though there is research into the area of the victims' lives such as Neal Sheldon's excellent books. In terms of respecting them I think modern day ripperology does respect the memory of the victims and tries in most cases to avoid sensationalism."

"Perhaps not, but this certainly not unique to these crimes. The victims and their families are soon forgotten while attention is focused on the suspect or killer. I will say that a number of researchers have done an incredible job of documenting information on the lives of the JTR victims."

"Probably not. I think that the passage of time and the sensationalism surrounding the case makes us forget that the victims were real people."

"No, I think that the best part of Ripperologists pay their attention only to the case and sometimes lose contact with reality. They often do not remember that we are dealing with women murdered in such a terrible way."

"No, I have to say I don't think so. I shouldn't really go on about this too much, I have already had people have a go at me on the Casebook forum for saying it, but too many people are too flippant in regards to the victims. This is actually something I could write pages and pages about. But I'm not going to."

"No, they can get overlooked by the hype surrounding catching the killer. Also they can be romanticised which is also unfair to them."

Question 5: What do you think is the biggest misconception surrounding the case?

*The theme of last issue's **Ripper Notes** was "Madmen, Myths and Magic", and so with the myths element of this in mind that I asked this question about misconceptions that surround the case. Personally, I could think of a few, and it seems you could too!*

"That it has been solved. Or that it never happened and it was just a Sherlock Holmes type of story."

"The idea that Jack the Ripper is some kind of bogey man who didn't exist."

"That JTR was a person of privilege, member or associate of the royal family, protected by the police, or other conspiracy type theory. I can't help but believe that he was living in or near Whitechapel and could freely move about without attracting undue attention. Perhaps the only surprising thing about his identity would be how nondescript, little known, and 'just like the quiet guy next door' he would be."

"I would have to say the image of the Ripper being a doctor with top hat and Gladstone bag walking through the fog."

"Amongst the public at large, that the murders had anything to do with the Duke of Clarence, or James Maybrick. Amongst Ripperologists, I think that too many people accept as fact that this was one person acting alone. It may have been – but there are plenty of reasons to think that it may not have been."

"The idea that someone, either the police at the time or someone since then, has already solved the case and that the rest of us are just too stubborn or stupid to appreciate the truth of the matter."

"I'd have to say that Jack was responsible for a greater number of murders is a big misconception that the general public have!"

"The grapes and the coins not found but believed to be found in Hanbury Street, near or under the body of Dark Annie."

"Organs removed were random acts and by a non-medical man, in the Eddowes case."

Question 6: What do you think the biggest step forward in Ripperology has been?

It's nice to end on a positive note. So here is one! It's nice to think of Ripperology as a developing field, where advances can be made. That we have something more than they had in the past to go on. Here are your thoughts:-

"The declassifying (if you like) of the Home Office and Police files and their publication to us the unwashed masses."

"I believe the 1988 return of Mary Jane Kelly's second photo and the Dear Boss letter. It gives us hope that there are other items out there waiting to be discovered."

"I would say that the internet age has been both a help and hindrance to Ripperology. Certainly it is a step forward in that sites like the Casebook and JTR Forums now exist where help is always at hand and discussions on obscure Ripper issues can be had from the comfort of one's own armchair."

"I am going to cheat and answer this with two things: The internet, especially sites like Casebook: Jack the Ripper which has made material so readily available to almost everyone. And the quality of work produced and completed by a core group of JTR researchers, truly incredible when one considers the age of the case."

"A move in recent years towards demanding factual correctness ahead of a good story."

"Cleaning the history of the crime from all the rubbish accumulated in over 100 years."

"Probably when authors like Rumbelow, Harris and Begg made a concerted effort to try to sort out the actual facts of the case from the legends that had been built up over the years from faulty newspaper reports and hoaxers."

"With two magazines of mainstream or better quality, hopefully 'non-Ripperologists' will be attracted to the case by their professionalism. Another is the seriousness of many of the people involved, almost to the point of trading punches! As much as the field needs reserved and scholarly individuals analyzing the case, it needs passionate repartee and viewpoints from every angle."

So concludes this issue's Inquest. Here are the questions for April:

Question 1: Has studying the Ripper case helped enhance your knowledge about the social conditions of Victorian England?

Question 2: Would determining which of the Whitechapel Murders were committed by the same person help identify the Ripper?

Question 3: Are speculations made in the press around the time of the murders about the identity of the Ripper helpful today?

Question 4: How helpful to us today are the statements made by police officials back then naming Ripper suspects?

Question 5: Do you think that if Ripperologists spent more time working together and less time arguing that we would be nearer to knowing the killer's identity?

As always, answers are totally confidential. Give as long or short of a response as you wish, and feel free to skip any question. Please respond by the first of March.

*You can send your answers by email (to **rippersurvey@yahoo.co.uk**), over the web (via **www.rippernotes.com/inquest.html**) or by regular postal mail (see page one of this issue for the address).*

Loretta Lay Books

Barnard (Allan) *The Harlot Killer* p/b signed £50

Begg (Paul) *Jack the Ripper The Facts* hb/dw new signed label £20

De Locksley (Dr. John) *The Enigma of Jack the Ripper* A4 softcover £35

De Locksley (Dr. John) *Jack the Ripper Unveiled* A4 softcover £35

Easdown/Sage *Jack the Ripper In A Seaside Town* signed, numbered p/b new £25

Evans/Skinner *Jack the Ripper Letters From Hell* hb/dw 2 signed labels £20

Evans/Skinner *The Ultimate Jack the Ripper Sourcebook* hb/dw 2 signed labels £25

Feldman (Paul H.) *Jack the Ripper The Final Chapter* hb/dw signed label £15

Hodgon (Peter) *Jack the Ripper Through the Mists of Time* p/b new signed £50

Leeson (Ex-Det-Sgt.) *Lost London* hb/dw £75

Linder/Morris/Skinner *Ripper Diary The Inside Story* hb/dw signed by all 3 authors £20

Macnaughten (Sir Melville L.) *Days Of My Years* h/b £125

O'Dell (Robin) *Jack the Ripper in Fact and Fiction* hb/dw signed label £65

O'Donnell (Elliott) *Great Thames Mysteries* h/b £125

Osher 583 (Frater Achad) *Did Aleister Crowley Know the Identity of JtR?* booklet new £35

Paley (Bruce) *Jack the Ripper The Simple Truth* softcover £30

Punch, Or the London Charivari Vol. 95 1888 h/b Mint £150

Punch, Or the London Charivari Vol. 95 1888 h/b Nr. Vg. £100

Rumbelow (Donald) *The Complete Jack the Ripper Fully Revised & Updated* new p/b signed label £9

Sugden (Philip) *The Complete History of Jack the Ripper* hb/dw ex-lib £20

Turnbull (Peter) *The Killer Who Never Was* h/b £200

Wolf (A.P.) *Jack the Myth* hb/dw £125

Wolff (Camille) *Who Was Jack the Ripper? A Collection of Present-Day Theories & Observations* hb/dw new with 14 signatures £130

Mail Order Only

24 Grampian Gardens.
London NW2 1JG
Tel 020 8455 3069
mobile 07947 573 326

www.laybooks.com

lorettalay@hotmail.com

Other items:

Video: *Hands of the Ripper* £5

Video: *Jack the Ripper* (Caine/Seymour/Collins) £5

Video: *The Secret Identity of Jack the Ripper* (Ustinov/Leeming) £5

Video: *Jack the Ripper The Final Solution* £5

Video: *The Diary of Jack the Ripper: Beyond Reasonable Doubt* £5

Jack the Ripper Pub Sign approx. 14" x 10" £15

News & Notes

By Dan Norder

Attack of the 110 year old Ripper

A couple of months back a number of Australian newspapers printed articles that said the first "Reclaim the Night" protests (called "Take Back the Night" in the U.S.) were started in England as a response to the Jack the Ripper killings of... 1977?

Sure, sometimes people get the year wrong, but being off by 89 years is pretty amazing. That incredibly mixed up date apparently comes from confusing Jack the Ripper with the Yorkshire Ripper. I guess some people don't realize a number of killers went by similar names.

As far as that goes, organizers of the Australian Reclaim the Night events also don't seem to realize that the event actually originally started in Rome and then West Germany before going to England. Either that or they think it sounds better their way.

* * *

The better to hug you with, my dear

Mark Gatiss, while promoting his novel *The Vesuvius Club,* which mentions painter Walter Sickert, bristled at the suggestion that he was adapting plot points from the idea that the artist was Jack the Ripper.

"I can't bear the Patricia Cornwell thing," he told the *Guardian.* "It's my bete noire. First, because it's the oldest theory in the world. Second, Sickert was in France for the whole time the Whitechapel murders were happening. So unless he had very long arms, it wasn't him."

In the interest of fairness, we should point out that evidence suggests Sickert was in France for only most of the Ripper murders, not all of them. That's probably an understandable mistake.

More troubling is that Gatiss might be inadvertently putting ideas into people's heads. After all, Cornwell managed against all historical evidence to convince herself (and many of her readers) that Sickert had a fistula on his penis that made it impossible for him to have normal sexual relations. It wouldn't be difficult for her to incorporate another alleged deformity into the next edition of her book. The long arm theory may yet gain legs.

Mark Gattis

From a publicity photo.

* * *

Ripper toy causes controversy

Last time around we made brief mention of a new Jack the Ripper figure being released by Mezco Toyz. Since then it has been released in two different styles, attracting negative publicity in the process.

The fully articulated toys come in two versions: one with a bowler hat and a large grimacing face displaying rotting teeth and the other with a top hat and a closed mouth. Both come with four assorted knives, a cleaver, syringe, a victim's removed uterus (yes, that's what it says), saw, medical bag (which opens to hold the other items) and a fabric trench coat.

The toys made headlines in Vancouver after family members of a missing prostitute believed killed by Robert William Pickton, who is is being charged with 15 counts of first degree murder, were appalled by their sale at the local Virgin Megastore.

Rogers Media Inc. reported in late December that Maggie DeVries, sister of the one of 31 women whose DNA was found at Pickton's farm,

Above: The Mezco Jack the Ripper figure that has a bowler hat and rotting teeth, in display box.

Left: The alternate version of the toy has a top hat and closed mouth, shown here with its coat removed and the various accessories spread out around it.

said, "In Vancouver in particular, they're not even that far from where the women disappeared from. We have a glimmer of how these women may have died. A doll with a bloodied hand, a bloody knife is way too close to home." DeVries wants Virgin to remove the toys from its shelves.

(And, as an aside, these news reports claimed that Jack the Ripper killed "about a dozen" victims. I wonder if they got that factoid off the toy or somewhere else.)

I'm not really surprised that there was some controversy, but I thought the Freemasons would be the first to complain, as initial images showed the medical bag as having a Masonic symbol. The new photos don't show this, but it's uncertain whether it was removed before production or if it's just on the other side of the bag in the press release images.

The figures are 10 inches tall, priced at $16 each, suggested for ages 15 years and older and available at a variety of stores or online via the **mezcodirect.com** website.

* * *

Ruthless editorials

Ramon Tulfo of the *Philippine Daily Inquirer*, in a November column about gays in the military, said, "I know a military officer who was a ruthless killer when he was still in the service. It turned out he's gay. Perhaps because he's gay, he's ruthless. Jack the Ripper, killer of many prostitutes in London in the 1800s, was said to be a homosexual."

I presume he's referring to Dr. Francis Tumblety there, but his homosexuality is generally considered a point against his candidacy as a suspect. Statistically speaking, gays aren't known for being particularly violent, of course. But then editorial columnists aren't known for being particularly concerned with making sense either.

* * *

More Ripper politics

After Palestinian Liberation Organization Chairman Yasser Arafat died, Ambassador Yoram Ettinger of Israel wrote in the *Washington Times* that the leaders of the Palestinian Authority should not be accepted uncritically.

"Legitimizing top leaders of the PA, such as Abu Mazen, Abu Ala', Dahlan and Rajoub – in defiance of their horrific track records – constitutes a victory of wishful thinking over moral clarity," Ettinger said. "The suggestion that the four are moderate compared with Mr. Arafat, is to suggest that the Boston Strangler was moderate compared with Jack the Ripper."

Yasser Arafat

* * *

Abberline grave project progress looks promising

Robin Lacey's exploration (as first mentioned in the July 2004 issue) of the possibility of getting a headstone to put on Frederick Abberline's grave seems to be advancing. Reportedly someone on the Bournemouth Town Council has now become involved.

We'll keep you updated on the latest as we hear about it.

* * *

Ripper's roommate saved millions of people from certain death

If someone were to tell you that he was responsible for having saved the world and that he lives in a small apartment with Jack the Ripper, you might understandably think he was crazy. But there is one man who can honestly say those things about himself.

In 1983, Stanislav Petrov was the commander in charge of a Soviet Union bunker that ran an early warning defense system for that country. A satellite array reported that five nuclear missiles were heading for Moscow. Regulations required alerting superiors so they could launch a full counterattack, but Petrov couldn't understand why the United States would only fire five missiles. He chalked it up to a false alarm and recommended no response.

Luckily for everyone, Petrov turned out to be right. The satellite had misread sunlight reflecting off clouds over a Montana military site as rockets being fired.

Oh, and that living with Jack the Ripper thing? That's the name of his dog, according to a December report from the Knight Ridder news service.

* * *

It's probably friends with Kangaroo Jack...

According to a December report in the *Korea Herald*, a crocodile in the Koala & Wildlife Park of Kuranda, Australia, has been named Jack the Ripper after it attacked 12 girls.

If that's true it's kind of surprising that they let it remain there. I suppose it makes a nice conversation piece for the tourists. If it were me, though, I'd use something I picked up from watching Disney's *Peter Pan*: Crocodiles with pocket watches in their stomachs can't sneak up on people as easily. If only there were a watch out there that would be appropriate to feed to a reptile that goes by the name Jack the Ripper...

* * *

What watch? Ten watch. Such much?

The reports of the tests on the alleged Maybrick watch a decade back have now been publicly released.

For those who are unaware of this entire episode, a short summary goes something like this:

A photo album with pages torn out was found which contained several pages of text claiming that the author was James Maybrick and that he was responsible for the Jack the Ripper murders. Shortly after, a women's pocket watch that had etchings on it claiming that it belonged to Maybrick and that he was Jack was announced as having been found. Both items led to quite heated debate.

The authors of the reports concluded that the scratched letters on the watch were at least "tens of years old." Proponents of its authenticity say that makes the theory that the watch was purposefully inscribed with the words after the Maybrick/Ripper diary became public impossible. Those supporting the idea that it was done recently say that the tests were inconclusive, while others believe the watch scratches could be both old and a hoax. The three sides have renewed their arguments with great emotion.

The general content of the reports has been known for a long time, though you wouldn't know that from some muddled news reports calling the tests "new" and "recent." One of the more amusing ones came from *The Llewellyn Journal* (by the publisher of *Fate* magazine), which claimed that the tests were done recently, repeatedly called Maybrick "Mayfair" and tried to use astrology to determine the Ripper's nature ("the murderer was someone who visited the neighborhood a lot, but who didn't live there" and "had a hatred of and fear of sex") all in the same article.

The watch reports can be seen online at the *Casebook: Jack the Ripper* site. Here's a shortcut to the page: **http://tinyurl.com/4hsze**

* * *

Ripper 2 going nowhere fast

Ripper 2: Letter from Within, the 2003 direct-to-video sequel to the lackluster 2001 movie *Ripper: Letter from Hell*, is still looking for a distributor to take it on. Considering the kinds of dreck that regularly makes it to video rental outlets, this almost has to be proof that *Ripper 2* is exceedingly bad.

As far as I've heard, so far it has only been released in the Netherlands. If anyone there saw it, none of them are willing to admit to it, judging by the lack of information about it that I can find anyway.

* * *

A holly just for jolly Christmas

Matt Tiabi of the alternative *New York Press* newspaper seemed to be attempting to outdo both Ebenezer Scrooge and Jack the Ripper (not to mention apparently wanting to try to undo what Stanislav Petrov had accomplished) when he wrote:

"Christmas is the world's most compelling argument for immediate nuclear attack against the territory of the United States. American Christmas makes heroes of Osama bin Laden, Jim Jones, the Shining Path, the Baader-Meinhofs, Jack the Ripper and the virus that causes AIDS. [...] Die waiting for Santa Claus to come down that chimney. He is not coming. But I am – to eat your corpse."

Yeeouch. Somebody obviously never got that train set he wanted from Santa when he was a kid...

* * *

Recent and upcoming publications

Christopher J. Morley's self-published *Jack the Ripper 150 Suspects* has been released. See the review starting on p. 113 of this issue for more information.

Neil Storey's *A Grim Almanac of Jack the Ripper's London 1870-1900* (ISBN 0-7509384-4-7, £17) also came out, but when Wolf Vanderlinden asked Sutton Publishing about it, the contact person there had never heard of it, which isn't encouraging.

Jekyll and Hyde Dramatized: The 1887 Richard Mansfield Script and the Evolution of the Story on Stage (McFarland & Co., ISBN 0-7864187-0-2) by Martin A. Danaha and Alexander Chisholm came out and has been getting good reviews .

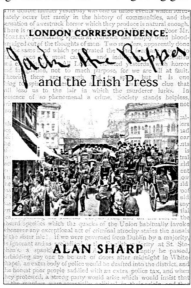

London Correspondence: Jack the Ripper & The Irish Press by Alan Sharp is on track for its scheduled February release from Ashfield Press (ISBN 1-901658-45-7, £12.50, CDN$29, $24). This book uses contemporary Irish press reports to study the social background to the murders. It features a history of key police officials and their anti-Fenian government activities, previously unseen stories and anecdotes from the streets of Whitechapel (including a vivid description of the dock fires on the night of the Mary Ann "Polly" Nichols murder), and a description of visiting Mary Kelly's room with the inquest jury.

I've seen a draft of the contents, and it looks like a must-have. We plan on reviewing it in the April issue of *Ripper Notes*.

Blake Publishing Ltd. has announced *Jack the Ripper: The Forensic Profile* by Trevor Marriot (ISBN 1-8445410-3-7, £18) which promises to reveal "a completely new suspect with unique access to the area of the murders," which should be interesting. It's scheduled for release on April 1.

No news yet on the upcoming books by Robert J. McLaughlin, Richard Whittington-Egan, Dr. Anna Gruetzner Robins, Peter Leek, Chris George, Tom Slemen or David Anderson. We'll keep you updated.

The Bookcase

By Wolf Vanderlinden and Dan Norder

Note: Each review ends with the initials of the editor who wrote it.

* * *

2005 "At Home" Edition of *Casebook: Jack the Ripper*

Type: Website on CD-Rom or DVD
Publisher: *Casebook: Jack the Ripper*
Release date: Winter 2004/2005
List Price: $19.99 ($23.48 with shipping)

I would imagine that if you are reading this publication then it is safe to say that you are interested somewhat in the "Great Victorian Mystery." If you are interested then you have no excuse not to log on to **www.casebook.org** and peruse what is an invaluable resource: the website of *Casebook: Jack the Ripper*. For those of you who haven't, shame on you. For those of you who can't, for whatever reason, here is the next best thing: the 2005 "At Home" Edition of the *Casebook*.

The "At Home" version is virtually the same as the actual website except that you cannot use the message boards. You can, however, read all the message boards that are archived from November 1996 up to winter 2004/2005. This allows you to read and re-read all those stimulating messages on the Diary boards or spend a fun filled evening at home attempting to figure out exactly what David Radka's A?R theory is really all about.

Perhaps cerebral meltdown is not what you would consider a fun time? You also have access to the hundreds of newspaper files from around the world that are archived in the Press section, as well as other invaluable resources. This part of the *Casebook* is the real reason why you should own a copy of the "At Home" edition.

The CD-Rom version is loaded onto the hard drive and unfortunately eats up 1.1 gigabytes of space, but it means that you never have to log on to the internet in order to access all the information. Fantastic if you have no internet connection. You can also take it with you anywhere, which is a plus if you regularly take your laptop to the library or class.

Also, a new feature with the 2005 edition is that it comes with a search engine which is incredibly handy, as those of you who have the old version can attest, but note that you need the Java VM module in order to run it. Even without the search engine this edition seems much easier to navigate through than the old one.

If you already own an old copy of the *Casebook* CD-Rom you should think about updating for several reasons. One is you will be receiving all the new newspaper files that have been added during the course of the year. Another is a year's worth of the new messages on the message boards, if that turns your crank. But the real reason that you should buy the 2005 edition is that by doing so you are supporting *Casebook: Jack the Ripper*, which is an incredibly worthy thing to do, especially if you have ever logged on, posted a message or made use of its free resources.

Highly recommended.

-W.V.

* * *

Jack the Ripper 150 Suspects

Christopher J. Morley

Type: Softcover, Nonfiction
(limited to 100 copies)
Length: 204 pages
Dimensions: 5.75" wide x 8.25" tall
Publisher: Self-published
Release date: December 2004
Can be purchased via:
christopherjmorley@hotmail.com
List Price: £20.00 (includes shipping)

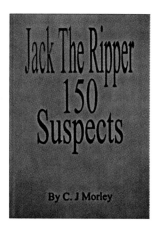

Book of Jack the Ripper suspects: take two.

Once more I am reminded of how great an idea this concept is: a book dedicated exclusively to the various men and women (but not, sadly, the "large ape" that one woman from the Isle of Wight suggested) who have been accused of being the Ripper. Once more I am struck by the possible importance of such a book for researchers or the merely Ripper curious. A book that can stand next to the *A to Z* or the *Ultimate Sourcebook* on the library shelf. Author Chris Morley, who also recently published *Jack the Ripper - Eliminating the Suspects,* comes close but doesn't quite reach this height.

The book lists, not surprisingly, 150 suspects and runs from the Malay cook Alaska to a Polish Jew named Wirtofsky. The entries are, for the most part, short, with some only a paragraph in length, while a longer look is taken at some of the more famous names. Unfortunately the author adds his own opinions about the viability of many of the suspects and dismisses several because they either do not match an un-sourced witness description (apparently by Israel Schwartz) of a short, stout man while supporting others simply because they have some medical knowledge. An unbiased look at the suspects would have been preferable, in my opinion.

Be that as it may, Morley wisely includes absolutely everyone he can find who has had the finger of guilt pointed at him (or her). The identification may be ludicrous or the suspect may have been exonerated by the police or history, but at one time or other, proof or no proof, each of these names has been offered as being that of Jack the Ripper. Therefore, alongside more famous suspects as Druitt, Kosminski, Maybrick and Sickert etc., the author has given us the names of people who drunkenly staggered into police stations and confessed (William Bull), were arrested for carrying suspicious parcels or bags (Oliver Mathews) or who aroused suspicion by just looking at someone funny in a pub (Arthur Henry Mason). This is the strength and importance of this book: although it is not complete, it is comprehensive. This allows the legitimate inclusion of such suspects as Frederico Albericci (who no one has been able to prove existed), M.J. Trow's non-suspect Frederick Charrington and Jonathan Goodman's fake suspect Peter J. Harpick (an anagram for Jack the Ripper). Morley also doesn't pad his book and offers only one entry for Dr. Frederick Richard Chapman (a.k.a. Dr. Merchant) and one for Ernest Dowson (a.k.a. Mr. Moring). This makes for a more logical entry on these suspects and thus is less confusing to the newbie. The book also seems to be fairly current with the inclusion of such recently discovered names as Tom Slemen's Claude Reigneir Conder, American murderess Elizabeth Halliday and Michael Conlon's Arbie La Bruckman.

Now for the bad news.

La Bruckman, for example, is found not in the L's but in the B's and for some reason Morley calls him "Bruckman" in the body of his account but lists the name correctly in the header. Also, although there is about a paragraph of information on this suspect, the rest of the two page entry is mainly a retelling of the Carrie Brown murder. The author thus has more to say about Ameer Ben Ali, the man who was arrested and charged with this murder, than La Bruckman. Worse, some of the information is incorrect. Here, then, is the major flaw in this book: it has several errors.

Some are errors in the spelling of names. Assistant Police Commissioner James Monro is listed as "James Monroe" while Levitski, the supposed accomplice to Ripper suspect Dr. Pedachenko, is listed as "Letvitski," for example.

Many are errors in facts. For instance, Michael Kidney and Elizabeth Stride did not live at 35 Dorset Street, and Kidney did not keep Stride padlocked in their room. This type of error comes from the careless use of secondary sources, and, although annoying, they don't really affect the merits, pro and con, of Kidney's candidacy for being the Ripper. Unfortunately, however, errors – such as stating that Kidney walked into Leman Street Police Station to harangue the police before the body of Stride was even identified – do.

Morley uses this episode to suggest that Kidney may have known that Stride was the unidentified victim because he had killed her. Thus this is evidence that Kidney might have been the Ripper. In reality the police had been given the name Elizabeth Stride, but were unable to positively identify the body as being hers, and the newspapers had already published Stride's name before Kidney drunkenly staggered into the Leman street nick on the evening of the 1st of October. Unfortunately it is these errors which prevent this book from becoming an important research tool.

The fact that Christopher Morley has written a handy book with 150 suspects listed is to be commended. His entries are not as in-depth as the 70 in Stan Russo's book *The Jack the Ripper Suspects*, for those who wonder about a comparison (and let me point out that Russo's book is also not without several errors), but he makes up for this with comprehensiveness and a reasonable price for his book. Do I recommend *Jack the Ripper 150 Suspects*? Yes I do, but with a caution.

-W.V.

* * *

RipperOpoly: Whitechapel Edition

John Jackson and Tim Mandese

Type: Board game
Dimensions: 10.5" x 10.5" x 2" (box)
Publisher: Self-published
Release date: October 2004
Can be purchased via: **RipperOpoly.com**
List Price: $48 (includes shipping to the U.S.) or $60 (with international shipping)

This product is really simple to explain: it's a knock off of the *Monopoly* game but with a Jack the Ripper theme. *Monopoly* clones are pretty popular. There are all sorts of variations out there, from the marketing tie-ins – *Star Wars Monopoly*, for example – to the regional variants. Around where I live we have at least three of those that I know of: *Wisconsinopoly*, *Madisonopoly* and *Moooo-nopoly*, after the dairy cows on the farms not too far away. (Yes, I obviously live in a hot spot of cultural sophistication, so sue me). But the question in this case is does the concept work with a theme based upon a serial killer?

A RipperOpoly game piece on the board.

My first concern when I heard about the concept was that it would end up completely hokey or tasteless. I think the makers of *RipperOpoly* have managed to do a pretty decent job of avoiding those pitfalls. When you first pull out the pieces and see the skull in place of the single dot on the dice or the skulls in top hats that serve as player tokens, you might worry that this could end up glorifying the killings, but the game play doesn't go that route at all. You've got properties taken from the case that you can buy to make doss houses on. You can charge more if a player lands on the space you bought if you had all of the same color and bought barrels or mugs for them. The railroad spaces from the original game are now pubs and the utilities are police stations. It's basically just harmless fun.

The production quality of the game is pretty impressive. The board folds out to a standard size, and it's made of a sturdy material with graphically impressive little pictures on many of the spaces. Of course it is fairly expensive, so at that price you should expect a glossy color game board and nice little tokens. The instruction sheet and the cards for the newspaper and police file spaces are somewhat low frills, but those are the two components that it matters the least on.

If you think it would be fun to have a Jack the Ripper-themed version of the game of *Monopoly,* then this is something you obviously should get, because the production standards are worth it. If that idea doesn't appeal to you, then, no, don't get it. Simple, eh?

There's one last thing possibly worth mentioning here. The game box and the website both call this the "Whitechapel Edition," but I'm not sure why. I don't know if that means other editions will be coming later or what. If there's a *RipperOpoly: Star Wars Edition* I hope they let you kill that annoying Jar Jar Binks character. I bet people would buy it based upon that alone. On the other hand, *RipperMooo-poly: Mad Cow Edition* might sell better where I live.

-D.N.

* * *

Ripperologist issue #56

The November 2004 *Ripperologist* celebrated its 10th anniversary by devoting most, though not all, of the issue to articles about the Ripper case. It was a welcome change after the recent dry spell during which the editors and authors seemed to have forgotten the name of the magazine.

This time around we had articles from Robin Odell on the sociological changes the Jack the Ripper murders caused, Tom Wescott on why he thinks Robert D'Onston Stephenson makes a good candidate for having written some of the more famous letters that claimed to have been written by the killer, John Savage on his research in tracking down some bit players mentioned in the most famous Royal Conspiracy theory, Nina Thomas on the possible use of the thimble that was found on Catherine Eddowes' body, Jennifer Pegg on why people are still debating the issue of the alleged Maybrick/ Ripper Diary and Stan Russo on... how every person ever named as a suspect is just as deserving as every other one? (Would that mean that my theory that Diddles the Kitten was the killer is worth a book?) Or maybe that's not what he was trying to say and I'm just confused.

And the standard Ripper content – news briefs, newspaper clippings, and so forth – was also there.

Oddly enough though, the piece specifically meant to cover *Ripperologist*'s decade of publication didn't really talk about the magazine that much. It instead focused to a large extent on which buildings from the Victorian era still exist in the East End of London. Granted, the point was brought up because the first issue of the publication discussed the topic, but once it was mentioned it kind of took over the article. The lack of discussion of anything that happened in those ten years between the first issue and this most recent one really stood out by its absence.

After having given the editors a bit of a hard time about the lack of Ripper-related content in recent issues, I was somewhat shocked to discover that my favorite article this time around had absolutely nothing to do with Jack. I wasn't even sure I was going to bother to read European Editor Eduardo Zinna's piece on music hall performer Dan Leno when I first saw it, but I ended up finding it quite interesting. I don't buy the arguments that were posted on the *Casebook: Jack the Ripper* message boards afterward that it has any relevance to the Ripper murders, but an occasional tangent is fine as long as it's written well. Oh, and provided there are other articles that are on topic, which this issue certainly had.

Here's hoping they keep it going for future issues.

-D.N.

Do you have a book or other Ripper-related product that you'd like to see reviewed here? You can mail it to the address on page 1 or email for more information.

The Whitechapel Letterbox

Well wishes from the previous editor of *Ripper Notes*

Dan -

I had held off on writing to you after your first issue of *RN,* as I know how difficult it is to get things up and running. However, I just received issue 20 in the mail, and am writing to tell you how absolutely wonderful it is. You've got great writers, as well as a layout and graphics format I'd have killed for!

It's an enormous comfort to me to see the old girl is as strong as ever, and I wish you all the best. You've done a grand job, and I congratulate you.

I'm very happy to see you were able to get Paul and Bernard's articles at last. Please also send my congratulations to Wolf on his assumption of Associate Editor status.

All the best,

Christopher-Michael DiGrazia

Got something you'd like to let us know? Send a letter to the editor. All correspondence will be considered confidential unless you specifiy that it is intended for the Whitechapel Letterbox. Letters may be edited for punctuation, grammar or length.

Address:
  Dan Norder, *RN* editor
  2 N. Lincoln Ridge Dr.
  Apt. #521
  Madison, WI 53719

Email address: **dan@norder.com**

The Facts author responds

Dear Dan,

Many thanks for the review of my book *Jack the Ripper: The Facts* in the last issue of *Ripper Notes* – another fine issue, I might add – and I'd appreciate it is you and any readers would let me know the errors you find so that I can correct them if the book goes into paperback. You take issue with me on three points and whilst I don't usually respond to criticism in reviews, I hope you won't be offended if I do so in this instance as I think they raise interesting topics that might generate further discussion and discoveries. I can't comment on the police statements to which you referred (hopefully it wasn't Anderson, who I took great pains to explain in detail) because you didn't specify them, but allow me to clarify the Annie Chapman and P.C. Long criticisms.

I said Annie Chapman was drunk when she left the lodging house because we're told she had been drinking beer, because we're told it didn't take much to get her intoxicated and because we're told by two sources that she was drunk when she left to find her lodging money. However, I acknowledge Dr. Phillips' contradictory medical evidence on page 80 of *Jack the Ripper: The Facts,* where I point out that at the inquest he specified 'strong alcohol', a term usually applied to spirits and not beer, from which I deduce that she was drunk on beer and that it had either passed through her system or was not looked for or mentioned by Dr. Phillips.

According to the inquest testimony – see *The Daily Telegraph* 12 September 1888 for a good account – the night watchman,

John Evans, saw Chapman come into the lodging house soon after 12.00 midnight and she sent one of the lodgers for a pint of beer. This was possibly William Stevens (erroneously given as Frederick Stevens in *The Star*) who said he drank a pint of beer with her at about 12.30. (see *The Star*, 8 September 1888). Chapman then went out again and returned shortly before a quarter to two. Timothy Donovan was sitting in his office which faced the front door and he saw Chapman go past and down to the kitchen. John Evans' wife was in the office with him and he asked her to find her husband and send him downstairs to ask Chapman for the money for her bed. Chapman, who was eating potatoes, came up to the office followed by Evans and said, 'I have not sufficient money for my bed. Don't let it. I shan't be long before I am in.' She left the house. Asked if she was drunk, Donovan said, 'She had had enough; of that I am certain. She walked straight. Generally on Saturdays she was the worse for drink. She was very sociable in the kitchen. I said to her, "You can find money for your beer, and you can't find money for your bed." She said she had been only to the top of the street – where there is a public-house.' John Evans testified that she 'was the worse for drink, but not badly so' and said that 'before he spoke to her about her lodging money she had been out for a pint of beer.' (see *The Times*, 11 September 1888 for Evans' statement that she had been for a beer.)

We know that it didn't take much for Chapman to get drunk because we have the testimony of he friend Amelia Palmer/ Farmer, who told the inquest that Chapman 'could not take much drink without getting intoxicated.' (*The Star*, 10 September 1888)

Against this we have the testimony of Dr. George Bagster Phillips, who was asked at the inquest if there was any appearance of Chapman having taken 'much alcohol' and replied, 'No. There were probably signs of great privation. I am convinced she had not taken any strong alcohol for some hours.' (*The Daily Telegraph*, 14 September 1888)

Dr. Phillips' testimony is at variance with the testimony of at least three witnesses that Chapman had been drinking beer. An explanation is therefore necessary and I suggest that whilst there was no evidence of Chapman having taken 'much alcohol' – and it didn't take much to get her tipsy – Dr. Phillips was looking for 'strong alcohol', namely spirits, not beer. Beer was still considered nutritious and part of a healthy diet in 1888 and a licence wasn't even needed to sell it, as was the case with spirits, and unlike licensed pubs, beer houses like the Britannia weren't shown on Ordnance Survey maps. My conclusion was also reached by *The Daily Telegraph* (27 September 1888), or the news agency from which it took the story, which reported, 'it was probably only malt liquor that she had taken, and its effects would pass off quicker than if she had taken spirits.' (I should add that Malt liquor meant beer, not a spirit like malt whisky. Pie and mash shops still refer to the parsley sauce as a liquor.)

I conclude that Annie Chapman had been drinking, that it didn't take a lot to make her drunk, that she was tipsy when she left the lodging house and that by the time of her death she had sobered up and the beer had passed through her system or wasn't looked for by Dr. Phillips.

(I might observe that although some evidence suggests that Elizabeth Stride had spent most of the evening drinking, Dr. Phillips was asked by a juror specifically 'Was there any trace of malt liquor in the stomach?' to which Dr Phillips answered, 'There was no trace.' Whether we take this to mean that Stride hadn't been drinking or that she had and it had passed through her system is for those with the appropriate knowledge to determine.)

Turning to the problem of the apron, when I wrote on page 181 that 'There was and *is* no doubt that Jack the Ripper passed through Goulston Street on his way from Mitre Square ...' I simply meant that there was and is no doubt that the piece of apron belonged to Eddowes and that the murderer dropped it where it was found. I did not mean to imply that the murderer went straight from Mitre Square to Goulston Street and never took a circuitous route to get there or stopped off anywhere in between (although I don't believe that he did). Whether or not I should have discussed the problem presented by P.C. Long's claim that the apron wasn't there when he passed through Goulston Street at 2.20 a.m., you're probably right that it deserved mention, probably as a footnote, but any discussion depends on how seriously you think it is that the apron actually wasn't there. We have inadequate descriptions of the piece of apron, but at the inquest P.C. Long said that 'one corner of was wet with blood' (inquest papers and newspaper reports; see *Daily Telegraph* 12 October). Otherwise Long said, 'there were blood stains on it, and one portion of it was wet' (the *Daily News* 12 October), and according to the testimony of Dr. Frederick Gordon Brown at the inquest, it was stained with 'some blood and apparently faecal matter' (Inquest papers). *The Daily Telegraph* (5 October) reported him as saying 'I fitted that portion which was spotted with blood ...' and *The Times* (5 October) reported Dr Brown as saying that 'there were smears of blood on one side as if a hand or a knife had been wiped on it.' Therefore, as far as we can tell, although one corner was wet with blood, the apron was not otherwise heavily stained with blood and had the appearance of *one side* having been used by someone to wipe their hand and/or knife. This wiping may also have deposited the faecal matter on the apron. We can therefore probably rule out the idea that the apron was used to carry the kidney and uterus because these would have deposited a greater quantity of blood on the material and left distinctive marks.

If the apron was simply used by the murderer to wipe his hands and knife, it is therefore something the murderer would have discarded as soon as he had finished with it. This conclusion is suggested by the fact that the apron was incriminating, had a corner wet with blood that could have got onto his hands and stained his clothing, and because the faecal matter was something the murderer would not have wanted to carry around with him for any length of time. If the apron was something the murderer used and would have quickly discarded, it follows that he did not hang around the murder scene or take a long and circuitous route to get to Goulston Street. It is also highly improbable that he would have reached home, then ventured out to the vicinity of the murder scene to dispose of an incriminating piece of evidence that he could have burned on the fire.

Thus, the condition of the apron suggests that the murderer went from Mitre Square, dropped the apron as he passed through Goulston Street and that it was there when P.C. Long passed through at 2.20 a.m. and that Long didn't see it.

(Let's not get into possible symbolism in the dropping of an apron and the recent Leather Apron scare, the apron from a victim being dropped below a chalked message referring in all probability to the Jews, lately the target for hostility because of Leather Apron, and the 'Dear Boss' letter referring to Leather Apron ... It's all too easy for one's brain to start hurting.)

Cheers,

Paul Begg

Printed in the United Kingdom
by Lightning Source UK Ltd.
130587UK00001B/107/A

9 780975 912928